POWER GAMES

A leader's guide to office politics and drama-free collaboration

ZOË ROUTH

For all those who long for a better world of work:
may you have the courage to bear the
torch and light the way.

PRAISE FOR *POWER GAMES*

Zoë has once again hit it out of the park! This, her latest book, is a smart, practical guide to navigating the power dynamics of the workplace. With insightful advice and real-world examples, it helps you tackle tough situations, manage challenging personalities, and stay ahead of the game.

Chantal Atkinson, General Manager Operations, CCS Group

What I love about this book is its immediate relevance to the real-world challenges all leaders face in dealing with power. It draws upon extensive research and experience, and translates this into practical insights and actions that you can use immediately. Anyone trying to create and sustain thriving teams and collaborations will benefit from the wisdom and pragmatism in this book.

Dr Bek Christensen, environment leader and coach

In *Power Games*, Zoë Routh paints a powerful picture of the dynamics at play in our workplaces. She calls out the factors that most commonly lead to the misuse and abuse of power but also provides us with valuable insights to grow our own expertise and competency and harness power to thrive personally, and positively influence, within these complex environments.

Dr David Cooke, author of *Kind Business: Values Create Value*

Power isn't the problem – how we use it is. In this book, Zoë Routh shows us how to replace politics and manipulation with trust and influence. *Power Games* is a must-read for anyone serious about creating high-performing, drama-free teams.

Simon Dowling, author of *Work with Me: How to Get People to Buy into Your Ideas*

Power is destructive when in the wrong hands with the wrong intentions. This book offers not just a critique of toxic power games but also a clear, actionable path toward healthier, more collaborative leadership. It's a must-read for anyone looking to upgrade their leadership skills.

Dr Sylvia Rohde-Liebenau, author of *Who's in Charge? Lead With Real Power and Create an Impact in a Chaotic World*

Leadership in any era demands both insight and acceptance of self, others and the environment in which we lead. Through *Power Games* – and her Four Spheres of Power – Zoë Routh offers a masterful framework for leaders to not only develop and hone their political acumen, but to also exercise that skill with humanity and compassion.

Commodore Peter Scott, CSC, RAN (retired), author of
Running Deep: An Australian Submarine Life

In an era where workplace dynamics can make or break organisational success, this insightful guide illuminates the hidden patterns of office politics while providing a clear roadmap for genuine collaboration. Leaders struggling with workplace tensions will find this an invaluable resource for building the kind of relationship-centred environments that drive both professional fulfilment and organisational success – making it essential reading for both emerging and experienced leaders.

Nick Tebbey, National Executive Officer, Relationships Australia

Power Games is a practical guide to wielding power ethically, and preventing its abuse that leads to toxic culture. With actionable frameworks for creating healthy organisational dynamics, it's a must read for senior leaders.

Colin D. Ellis, author of *Detox Your Culture: Deliver Results,
Retain Staff, and Strengthen Your Organization's Reputation*

What I loved about *Power Games* was its clear, actionable framework – the Four Spheres of Power – which provides a fresh and practical approach to handling influence, conflict and collaboration. Zoë Routh has created an insightful and empowering guide that helps people foster stronger relationships, build ethical influence and create environments – at work and in life – where trust and respect thrive. A must-read for anyone seeking to navigate power with confidence, clarity, and integrity.

Alison Percival, CEO, The Tradies

Power Games is a must-read for leaders navigating the complexities of influence, strategy and workplace dynamics. With her signature humour, insight and clarity, Zoë unpacks the hidden power plays that shape organisations, offering practical tools to lead with confidence and integrity. Zoë's brilliant and thought-provoking guide is a must-read for 'real' people seeking to elevate their leadership game with authenticity and integrity.

Sheryll Fisher, Managing Director, Outback Initiatives

Power Games in the workplace can be very complex, but in this book Zoë has delivered an easy read that is not only thought-provoking but also contains practical tips and tools to help leaders and teams.

Sharon (Stokeld) Tuffin, CEO, Karralika

Zoë Routh's *Power Games* clearly defines the complex human terrain we all face at work and in life. She highlights that the days of relying on classic leader expectations, heroic saves and beneficial paternalism are over – and that leveraging the collective brain power and energy of all of us is the path to success. The book is a must read!

Marty Strong, author of leadership books *Be Nimble*,
Be Visionary and *Be Different*

First published in 2025 by Inner Compass Australia Pty Ltd

© Zoë Routh
The moral rights of the author have been asserted.

All rights reserved. Except as permitted under the Australian *Copyright Act 1968* (for example, a fair dealing for the purposes of study, research, criticism or review), no part of this book may be reproduced, stored in a retrieval system, communicated or transmitted in any form or by any means without prior written permission. All inquiries should be made to the author.

A catalogue entry for this book is available from the National Library.

PB ISBN: 978-1-7638786-0-0
HB ISBN: 978-0-6488773-9-4

Project management and text design by Publish Central
Cover design, shadow archetypes and icons created by Lynne Cazaly

Disclaimer
The material in this publication is of the nature of general comment only, and does not represent professional advice. It is not intended to provide specific guidance for particular circumstances and it should not be relied on as the basis for any decision to take action or not take action on any matter which it covers. Readers should obtain professional advice where appropriate, before making any such decision. To the maximum extent permitted by law, the author and associated entities and publisher disclaim all responsibility and liability to any person, arising directly or indirectly from any person taking or not taking action based on the information in this publication.

CONTENTS

Introduction ix

Part I: Recognising power and the games people play

Chapter 1: The landscape of power 3

Chapter 2: Understanding power games 19

Part II: Developing the Four Spheres of Power

Chapter 3: Introducing the Four Spheres of Power 41

Chapter 4: Stoke your Cauldron of Courage: Be brave 55

Chapter 5: Accumulate more Coin: Be seen 61

Chapter 6: Develop your Conch: Be heard 75

Chapter 7: Use the power of the Crown wisely: Beware 89

Part III: Power Games in Archetypes

Chapter 8: The Elder and the Tyrant 103

Chapter 9: The Warrior and the Bully 115

Chapter 10: The Diplomat and the Manipulator 129

Chapter 11: The Guardian and the Fanatic 143

Chapter 12: The Pioneer and the Gambler 153

Part IV Building healthy power structures

Chapter 13: Healthy power structures in teams   163

Chapter 14: Healthy power structures in organisations   187

Chapter 15: Seven deadly sins of systems power abuse   203

Chapter 16: Speaking truth to power   209

What's next?   213

Appendix A: Sample Code of Ethics   215

Appendix B: Sample Code of Conduct   219

Appendix C: Collaboration handbook questions   225

Appendix D: Integrative decision-making in a holacracy   227

Further reading   229

Acknowledgments   233

About the author   235

INTRODUCTION

When I was in my early twenties, I recall telling my boss at the time about a difficult romantic relationship I was having.

'So, who wears the ring?' he asked.

I stood there, wiping the cafe counter, growing confused.

'In every relationship, one person wears the ring,' he explained. 'They have control. They care less about what happens while the other person tries really hard to keep the relationship going. You want to be happy? Wear the ring.'

While I thought his concept of a healthy relationship quite skewed, the image of the ring of power stayed with me.

JRR Tolkien, of course, made the 'one ring to rule them all' a central metaphor of power in his aptly named *The Lord of the Rings*. Tolkien's message through the epic adventure story was clear: no one person (or creature) should wear that ring and wield that much power; it sends them bonkers.

We see this insight play out in painful real time in politics and with techno-billionaires: too much power and money turns people impulsive, selfish and chaotic. [Insert your favourite maligned celebrity figure here as an example].

Our workplaces are also far from immune from the Power Games that come with any level of leadership. The use and abuse of power and the grasping for more power, are common dynamics in the workplace – and many of us are suffering because of them. A 2023 survey of US workers from The Conference Board revealed 'more than 1 in 4 workers (26 per cent) say toxic work culture is having an impact on their mental health'.[1] And according to Gallup's 2024 *State of the Global Workforce* report, 'Twenty percent of [the world's] employees experienced a lot of loneliness the previous day'.[2]

Back here in Australia, the Australian Workers' Union published their own gobsmacking findings: 'One in two Australian workers has experienced being bullied, harassed or exposed to conflict or inappropriate behaviour … just as many report unrealistic workloads, poor training and exposure to traumatic events'.[3]

An abundance of research from recent years shows just how prevalent power misuse and abuse is in workplaces. After millennia of working together as a species, we still haven't got power right. It continues to be both a coveted and perilous instrument of leadership.

Why this: Power Games are still way too popular

Have you ever had your idea stolen by someone else? Did it leave you fuming? Maybe you had fantasies of revenge on the culprit; maybe you even acted on those fantasies.

Or maybe you were in line for a promotion, hoping your good work would speak for itself, only to lose out to a brasher, less competent colleague. They were good at talking the talk, but you were better at walking the walk. Only no-one else seemed to notice.

If you've ever worked in a team and found yourself frustrated by office politics, this book is for you.

---

1. The Conference Board (2023), 'Survey: Mental Health Worsens for 34% of US Workers', The Conference Board, 29 May, www.conference-board.org/press/mental-healthor-worsens-US-workers.
2. Gallup (2024), *State of the Global Workplace: The Voice of the World's Employees*, Gallup, 2024 report, www.gallup.com/workplace/349484/state-of-the-global-workplace.aspx.
3. Australian Workers' Union (2023), '50% of Australian workers report being bullied on World Mental Health Day', AWU, 10 October, awu.net.au/national/news/2023/10/20054/50-of-australian-workers-report-being-bullied-on-world-mental-health-day/.

If you've ever led a team and become exasperated by the infighting, petty jealousies and protective behaviour of your direct reports, this book is for you.

If you've ever sat in a meeting, grinding your teeth as someone dominated the conversation, the leader ignoring certain voices and elevating others, this book is for you.

If you've ever been on a committee and known the angst that can come with competing agendas and what feels like self-interest driving the conversation, this book is for you.

If you've ever been on the receiving end of:

- *Undermining:* Someone subtly sabotaging your work or reputation so they appear more competent.
- *Withholding information:* A colleague keeping critical information from you or others to maintain control.
- *Credit stealing:* Someone taking credit for your ideas or work.
- *Playing favourites:* Your boss giving preferential treatment to certain individuals to create a power imbalance.
- *Gossiping colleagues:* A gaggle of your teammates spreading rumours to manipulate perceptions and alliances.
- *Micromanaging:* Your boss exerting excessive control over others' tasks to assert dominance.
- *Gaslighting:* A colleague manipulating you or others to make them doubt their own perception or memory.

… this book is for you!

These are but some of the Power Games – and actually the more-benign ones – that play out every day in organisations.

Why now: Collaboration is the future of leadership

Aside from relieving the personal misery that comes from being on the receiving end of toxic Power Games, we need to address our ability to wield and respond to power for other important reasons. And the time to do so is now.

We need collaboration in teams

Working with others is hard – and that's why silos emerge. Silos are a natural by-product of organisational structures in which teams hunker down and focus on their primary work responsibilities. Typically, people who work on similar projects in the business bond because of their affinity with the work. They may also have similar values perspectives and ways of working. Hence the mini tribes you find in organisations, such as the marketing department, the finance area, the delivery team and those show-ponies in sales.

Humans wanting to hang out with other like-minded people is natural. It feels comfortable and easy. But 'comfortable and easy' does not an innovative, pioneering organisation make. So how do we bring disparate humans and diverse stakeholders together to solve a common challenge, without treading on each other's toes, insulting one another or (more commonly) secretly judging and resenting each other?

When people come together, even with good intentions, Power Games arise.

We need a new type of hero story

We all love a good hero story. It's inspiring and aspiring at the same time. Someone to fly in and solve all our problems? Wonderful! Saves me the trouble and we're all off the hook. The hero will take care of it.

The challenge with the hero story is that it embeds a sense of learned helplessness: 'we can't do it for ourselves; we need the hero'. We give away our personal power to the illusory force of personality. And it is an illusion – the hero can no longer deliver the goods these days. Complexity, volatility and uncertainty pretty much negate the ability for any one human to show us the path through.

But what we really value in a hero story is the courage of the leader. The leader's courage inspires our own courage. We don't really want one person to save the day. We don't really want to lose our sense of agency, do we?

The hero myth is dead. That old leadership paradigm is long gone. Our world is far too complex for us to rely on a singular human to guide us through the wilderness to the Promised Land.

The truth is the more we see, the better we lead. Our motto as leaders ought to be, 'See more, lead better'. In working problems, more minds bring more magic. We need stories of collective heroes, solving problems together.

More people, however, also bring more power struggles.

We need collaboration to solve our challenges

If we are to solve common challenges, teams – and leaders – need to collaborate better. However, power and Power Games scupper our best collaborative efforts.

The future of leadership involves collaboration on a scale we have not seen previously. Organisations have long needed their team members to collaborate – on projects, and on delivery of products and services. Too often, this is more like cooperation than true collaboration. Collaboration is the coming together of diverse minds to solve a collective challenge or seek a potential opportunity. It's an art and a skill that is rarely taught explicitly. When done well, innovation abounds, creativity surges and a robust team environment creates a great place to work. More often than not, however, collaboration is more like protected self-interest, guarded sharing, jealous ambition and other surreptitious power plays.

And it's not just in organisations. Governments are applying more and more pressure on organisations to collaborate and consolidate their resources, particularly in the social good not-for-profit organisations.

Across industries, the need to collaborate has never been greater. Current challenges of climate change, food security, supply chain volatility and vulnerability invite collaborative solution-finding between competitors.

The way forward

Let's be clear. Power is a dangerous thing. It's energising, but also addictive. It can activate the best part of us and stoke the worst part of us. So we need to change our relationship with power. Rather than something to be feared, we need to know how to cultivate and harness power, and deploy it with grace.

If we are to have a better relationship with power, we need to understand the nature of power itself before we hope to rein in the Power Games.

To reform our experience of power in the workplace for better collaboration within and between organisations, we need to do three things:

1. Understand and harness our personal power.
2. Create structures and systems for the effective and supportive deployment of power.
3. Establish organisation-wide power control measures.

My aim through this book is to equip you with a map of the perilous territory of power and a compass to navigate the treacherous terrain.

I see power as nested holons. (A holon is an entity that functions as a whole itself but is also part of a larger whole entity.) How we use power as individuals affects how we use it in teams, and thus how we design and navigate organisations. We need the three-pronged approach to keep Power Games from becoming toxic – that is, we need sensible use of power by individuals, careful and well-managed power in teams, and organisations that build culture and systems designed to monitor and manage temptations to misuse power.

My intention is that you build awareness and skills from the personal realm to team settings to across your organisation. No matter where your leadership journey starts and stops, you have an opportunity to master power in a healthy productive way. Let's get into it.

A NOTE ABOUT THE FICTIONAL EXAMPLES

Throughout the book, I've included fictional examples to bring to life the ideas and challenges. The characters in these stories are from my *Gaia* books, a near-future climate science fiction techno thriller series. The examples are all set at the beginning of Gaia's spacefaring journey, before they leave Earth to build communities on the Moon. Central to the stories is the question, 'What kind of leadership do we need *now* for what's *next*?'

To add some context to these snippets, Gaia Enterprises, founded by Maja Garcia and Huw Chan, is an organisation that emerges when sea levels rise, tsunamis wipe out Sydney and other coastal cities, and temperatures inland make it impossible to live anywhere but close to the coast. So humanity is squashed into very narrow strips of land, requiring innovation in how we work, grow food and live. Enter the new industry of 'world design' focused on building close-knit, dense living habitats in re-purposed high-rises, underground in caves, under water and artificial floating islands. Ambitious nations and techno-billionaires want to extend human habitat to other planets, starting with a base on the Moon.

And here's a little bit about the characters:

- Aryanna Sharif: Techno-billionaire and founder of Aryanna Industries, and also Chair of the Lunar Commission.
- Claire Edwards: One of Maja's first world design students, and now the chief operating officer of projects and the world design training school.
- Huw Chan: Co-founder of Gaia Enterprises.
- Jonas Seaborn: A world designer turned engineer working on his famous parents' floating world, the *Sea Rover*.

- Lincoln Ellison: Techno-billionaire and founder of Spaceward Bound, a space-faring, asteroid-mining company.

- Madison Floyd: Former US fighter pilot turned trainer for Spaceward Bound.

- Maja Garcia: Co-founder of Gaia Enterprises.

- Serena Fox: A world designer who specialises in life support technology for underground and underworld habitats.

I am writing these novels to explore difficult leadership challenges through story. I've discovered that when people see and feel the challenges through the characters, the insights go deeper and can carry us further than analytical text alone. So, enjoy!

PART I

RECOGNISING POWER AND THE GAMES PEOPLE PLAY

Fundamentally, power involves the capacity to shape outcomes, decisions or behaviours through influence, control or authority. Power can be used benevolently and for the greater good, or it can be used to maintain control and extend personal interests – and this is where the Power Games can come in.

In this part, I provide an overview of the landscape of power, explaining its effects (good and bad), how it is changing and why it can be abused. Then, the fun really begins, as we jump into the Power Games and consider the games played by bosses and between colleagues.

CHAPTER 1

THE LANDSCAPE OF POWER

No doubt you already have some idea of what power means to you and in your workplace. Other, more formal, definitions of power exist, with ChatGPT providing the following:

> *Power is the ability to influence or control the actions, behaviours and decisions of others, or the course of events, or the allocation of resources through authority, resources, relationships or knowledge.*

In other words, power is getting stuff to happen, either by being nice or playing hard ball.

Power can also be applied in different contexts, such as:

- *Social and political power:* In politics, power refers to the ability of individuals or groups to achieve goals, shape policy and make decisions.

- *Organisational power:* In organisational behaviour, power is viewed as the capacity to affect the actions of others, often associated with one's position in the hierarchy, control over resources or access to critical information.

- *Interpersonal power:* Power also operates in personal relationships, where it can be defined as the ability to influence the thoughts, emotions and actions of another individual through charisma, emotional intelligence or persuasion.

What about 'personal power'? This is a realm unto itself because it deals with our capacity to choose our thoughts, manage our emotions and take courageous action. You can develop the capacity to feel powerful and be powerful in your own right. The effect of this kind of work is in developing presence, and it feeds into the other spheres of power, as I cover in more detail in the chapters in part II, where I discuss the Four Spheres of Power.

In this book, I will touch on personal power, but development suggestions are discussed elsewhere in my other books and resources (see, for example, *People Stuff: Beyond Personality Problems*). In this book, I mostly dive into the realms of interpersonal and organisational power.

Power, however, is very – well – powerful. We need to understand how this intoxicating experience affects us.

The effects of power

When we gain power, the effect on us can be absolutely crazy. The research is staggering. When individuals gain power, several changes occur in the brain that can affect behaviour and cognition. Let's look at some of the key effects – good and bad.

The good stuff

Power can have the following positive effects:

- *Power is energising:* When we feel powerful, we feel exhilarated and confident. Power gives us a boost and charges up our reward activation centre with flushes of dopamine. And dopamine is addictive. It encourages us to keep doing that particular activity to get more of that feel-good juice. That's why when we gain power, we don't want to lose it – or its dopamine-generating tendencies.[4]

- *Power increases orientation to action:* We feel more activated with power, and are more likely to take decisive action and pursue our goals assertively. This is partly because power can reduce inhibition and the fear of failure, encouraging risk-taking and proactive behaviour.

- *Power activates authenticity and liberation:* In their awesome book *The Power Code: More Joy, Less Ego, Maximum Impact for Women (and Everyone)*, Katty Kay and Claire Shipman's research shows that, 'Power activates, allows us to exercise our will, which also allows us to be more authentic, more of ourselves, more liberated. And that, multiple studies demonstrate, creates opportunity for joy'. In other words, we feel able to express our true selves more freely when we feel powerful. With fewer constraints and fears about repercussions, we may feel more authentic and less likely to conform to others' expectations.

- *Power boosts cognitive thinking:* Kay and Shipman also reveal power can enhance certain cognitive functions, such as executive function and strategic thinking. We can better focus on goals and make complex decisions. Downside? Over-confidence and potential underestimation of risks. (See the following section for more on the downsides of power.)

- *Power can help champion a better world:* Power can enable us to champion ethical behaviour and create a culture of

---

[4] 'And what about Power Poses?' I hear you ask. In Amy Cuddy's famous TED Talk ('Your body language may shape who you are'), she discusses a change in hormones through using these 'power poses' (a rise of testosterone and decrease in cortisol), making us feel more in charge. Over 12 years of controversy followed, as many researchers were unable to replicate these changes. The literature now suggests that even though negligent change in biochemistry might occur, significant change does occur in subjective feelings of power. In other words, if you do a power pose, you feel more confident and in control, regardless of biochemistry. So, power pose your little heart out. See Loncar, T (2021), 'A decade of power posing: where do we stand?', *The Psychologist*, 8 June, www.bps.org.uk/psychologist/decade-power-posing-where-do-we-stand for more in this area.

integrity. Leaders with power who are committed to ethics can influence their organisations to adopt fair practices, transparency and responsible decision-making, setting an example for others to follow. Ethical leaders, such as Patagonia's founder Yvon Chouinard, use their influence to promote sustainability and socially responsible business practices, showing how power can be aligned with ethical values to benefit the greater good.

- *Power can be used as stewardship:* When we view power as a responsibility rather than a privilege, we make more ethical decisions. We focus on the long-term wellbeing of our employees, customers and the environment, promoting fairness and equity in the organisation. And this can be externally certified through a mechanism such as the B Corp. Certified organisations and their leaders often use their power to prioritise social and environmental performance, treating power as a tool for positive change. Let's have more of this, please.

The not-so-good stuff

Used in the wrong way, power can also have the following negative effects:

- *Power reduces empathy:* Studies have shown that power can diminish a person's ability to empathise with others. This occurs because power reduces the capacity to see things from another person's perspective, because powerful individuals may become less attuned to others' emotions and experiences. The surge of biochemicals such as dopamine and testosterone reduces the ability to mirror other people, which is essential for empathy. Some researchers liken these reactions as similar to 'psychopaths or patients with frontal brain damage'.[5]

- *Power increases the potential for corruption:* Because of the dopamine party that comes with power, we may seek to retain

---

[5] Azab, M (2020), 'The brain under the influence of power', *Psychology Today*, 9 June, www.psychologytoday.com/au/blog/neuroscience-in-everyday-life/202006/the-brain-under-the-influence-power.

our power or gain more of it through corrupt means. This can lead to moral relativism, where we start to justify the means for the ends.

- *Power leads to moral disengagement:* With too much authority, and distance from the impact of our decisions, we may become detached from the consequences of our decisions. This can make it easier for us to justify unethical actions if we believe we are serving a higher goal. We end up overlooking the impact of our decisions on lower-level employees or stakeholders, believing that our power justifies certain actions, such as cutting corners or bypassing rules.

- *Power leads to a sense of entitlement:* All the mind-bending effects of power may lead us to believe we are above certain ethical norms. This can lead to behaviours such as taking advantage of resources, misusing funds or engaging in coercive tactics to maintain control. We might end up thinking something like, *Do I really need to put in the paperwork and get approval from the board to hire that attractive person? After all, I'm the boss ... I should be able to make my own hiring decisions ...* Or, maybe this: *I'll just use the company credit card to pay for my daughter's car repairs. I'll pay it back. I'm good for it. After all, I'm the boss here ...*

- *Power decreases sensitivity to stress, and this stresses others:* With power, we feel energetic and more in control of our environment, and this helps us deal better with stress or minimise our perception of it. What's not to like? Except that we may become blind to the taxing effect of stress, and less aware of the impact of the situation on others.

- *Power makes us more impulsive and uninhibited:* Again, the intoxicating effect of dopamine reduces our self-monitoring. This can lead to inappropriate and sometimes unethical behaviour – think increases in gambling, unwise flirtations, sexual innuendo with more junior people or doing stupid things like a strip-tease at the annual Christmas party.

Power is a hot commodity. We revel in it. We crave more of it. It enables us to accomplish amazing things, for ourselves and others. But its dark side can bring us undone.

The global business environment is changing power in the workplace

The changing dynamics of the global business environment, marked by technological advancements, remote work, sustainability focus and shifting power in emerging markets, are reshaping how people use power in organisations.

These shifts have influenced both formal power structures and informal power dynamics. The following sections outline how.

Workplaces

Here's how power is changing in our workplaces.

Decentralisation of authority

Digital transformations such as cloud-based tools and remote work have decentralised traditional power structures within organisations. Teams are becoming more autonomous, and decision-making is more distributed, diminishing the need for rigid hierarchies. This has meant leaders have needed to adopt more collaborative, flexible styles rather than top–down, command-and-control approaches.

Transparency and accountability

Transparency, driven by the rise of social media, whistleblower protections, and employee and stakeholder activism, has made transparency a social expectation of organisations. Leaders are increasingly held accountable by employees, customers and stakeholders.

Power is shifting from leaders who used to operate behind closed doors to a more open, accountable approach. Leaders now need to balance authority with transparency and responsiveness to stakeholders. Leaders who fail to adapt to this openness can lose credibility and influence.

Sustainability and social responsibility as power levers

As sustainability and social responsibility become central to corporate strategy, employees who champion these causes gain influence. Consumers, investors and even employees now demand that companies align with environmental, social and governance (ESG) values.

Leaders who embed sustainability into corporate decision-making are gaining influence, while employees who advocate for social responsibility initiatives, such as diversity, equity and inclusion (DEI), are being seen as valuable contributors to corporate culture and strategy. Inclusion, rather than exclusion, is now the more influential power tactic.

Geopolitical influence on corporate leadership

Global geopolitical shifts, such as the Australia–China trade tensions and regulatory challenges around data privacy, are influencing how leaders wield power. Companies need leaders who can navigate complex international regulations and geopolitical risks.

Leaders who understand international trade, cross-border regulations and geopolitical risks hold significant power as they guide companies through increasingly volatile global landscapes.

Work

Now let's consider how the changing nature of work is having knock-on effects on power.

Shifting workforce power dynamics

Remote work and the rise of the gig economy have changed how employees perceive power in the workplace. Turbo-boosted by the COVID-19 experience, workers have reaped the benefit of flexible work. Workers are now more mobile and less tied to single organisations, which gives them more power to demand flexibility and better working conditions, or to seek opportunities elsewhere.

While power sways between employer and employees depending on workforce market conditions, overall the expectations between employers and employees have shifted. Job security as a benefit is not the bargaining chip it once was, while workers with in-demand skills (especially in tech – see the next section) have more leverage in negotiating employment conditions.

Technological expertise as a source of power

The growing reliance on technology, particularly AI, data analytics and automation, has shifted power towards employees with specialised knowledge in these areas. Digital literacy and the ability to work with cutting-edge technologies have become key sources of influence.

Employees in IT, data science and cybersecurity hold increasing power in organisations because their expertise is critical for innovation and safeguarding business continuity. This has created new centres of power around digital transformation teams.

Centralisation of power around data

Digital tools such as AI enable employees with expertise in this area to make data-driven recommendations that influence critical decisions. Their influence can lead to a democratisation of decision-making, as insights from AI are accessible across different departments, but they also shift the power towards those who manage these tools and understand their outputs.

As AI tools become integral to decision-making, power is shifting towards those who control data and the technology that processes it. Employees in IT, data science and AI management roles gain more influence as they manage the infrastructure that collects, stores and analyses data. Long live the technogeeks!

The power to control organisational knowledge now rests with individuals who can leverage AI and data analytics, potentially creating new informal power centres in organisations. This challenges traditional hierarchies, as even mid-level employees in data-intensive roles may exert significant influence over critical business decisions.

Workers

Finally, let's look at the workers who are changing their ideas of power.

Increased importance of network power

In an interconnected and transparent world, network power (influence through relationships, persuasion and communication) is becoming more critical than ever. Leaders and employees are leveraging social power through networks and relationships to gain influence, rather than simply relying on their formal titles or roles.

In flatter organisational structures, leaders must cultivate trust, emotional intelligence and communication skills to maintain influence. Those who can build networks and leverage relationships across departments or regions gain informal power.

Collaborative and inclusive leadership styles

As businesses shift towards collaborative, purpose-driven models, leadership styles have evolved. Command-and-control leadership is losing ground to collaborative, inclusive and servant leadership, where power is shared rather than concentrated.

Leaders who share power with their teams, foster inclusivity and listen to diverse perspectives are gaining influence. Employees with strong collaboration and leadership skills, regardless of position, are also emerging as key influencers within organisations.

Leaders and employees must now navigate a more fluid and decentralised power landscape, emphasising relationships, expertise and adaptability. In other words, if you play nice, you'll go far.

We can't change human nature, but we can change human systems

The previous sections seem to make it sound like it's all coming up roses: less command and control, more shared power, all in a more transparent and accountable landscape.

Don't be lulled into a false sense of security. While conditions have changed, human nature really hasn't. And that means we'll still have the same old chestnuts of Power Games poking their ugly little heads up like weeds in our Garden of Eden. So you need to get a handle on these time-honoured dynamics and pluck the weeds of power-mongering as they arise, long before you step up to the more challenging game of collaboration in complex, uncertain contexts. I get more into the nitty-gritty of Power Games in the next chapter. For now, let's look at why they are so attractive.

Why people abuse power

So what is it about human nature and power? Are some people just narcissistic, psychopathic assholes? Well, yes.

About 6 per cent of the general population has narcissistic personality disorder,[6] and about 4 per cent of the population are functional (non-criminal) psychopaths.[7] So that means in an organisation of 100 people, you are likely to find four to ten people who are willing to play hard with Power Games. Yikes.

Aside from them, people abuse power for other common reasons. Here are some psychological, environmental and systemic factors that contribute to power abuse.

---

[6] See Stinson, FS, et al (2008), 'Prevalence, correlates, disability, and comorbidity of DSM-IV narcissistic personality disorder: Results from the Wave 2 National Epidemiologic Survey on Alcohol and Related Conditions', *The Journal of Clinical Psychiatry*, 31 July, www.psychiatrist.com/jcp/prevalence-correlates-disability-comorbidity-dsm-iv-narcissistic-personality-disorder-wave-2-nesarc/ for the details here.

[7] For more in this area, check out the awesomely named book *Snakes in Suits: When Psychopaths Go to Work*, by Dr Paul Babiak and Dr Robert Hare.

Insecurity and ego

Insecurity and ego can link in with power for the following reasons:

- *Low self-esteem:* Individuals who feel insecure about their abilities or position may misuse power to compensate for their perceived inadequacies. By controlling others, they may feel more competent or superior.

- *Ego and arrogance:* Those with inflated egos may abuse power to assert dominance, prove superiority or maintain their status. Power can amplify narcissistic tendencies, leading to a desire to be in control at all costs.[8]

Desire for control

A need for control can also influence the abuse of power:

- *Fear of losing control:* Some people abuse power out of a fear of losing control over situations, decisions or people. They may use manipulation, coercion or micromanagement to ensure they remain in charge.

- *Need for order:* Individuals who seek to impose order or structure, even if unnecessarily rigid, may abuse power to enforce compliance and maintain a sense of security for themselves.

Corrupting nature of power

Power can also change the way we think, in the following ways:

- *'Power corrupts':* As Lord Acton famously noted, 'Power tends to corrupt, and absolute power corrupts absolutely'. Research, like the work done by professor of psychology Dr Dacher Keltner – and discussed in his book *The Power*

---

[8] For more on the link between power and narcissism, see McSweeny, L (2018), 'It's official: Power creates a narcissist', Pursuit, University of Melbourne, pursuit.unimelb.edu.au/articles/it-s-official-power-creates-a-narcissist.

Paradox: How We Gain and Lose Influence – shows that power can reduce empathy and increase self-interest, leading individuals to act in ways that benefit themselves without regard for others.

- *Cognitive changes:* Studies in neuroscience from Dr Keltner, and others, suggest that power can actually alter brain function, leading to this diminished empathy, along with disinhibition and a skewed sense of risk and consequence. This can encourage unethical behaviour because individuals feel invulnerable. Dr Keltner describes this kind of effect as a type of brain damage as people lose their ability to mirror and empathise.[9]

Systemic and cultural reinforcement

The abuse of power can be magnified by the environments it operates in:

- *Lack of accountability:* In environments with few checks and balances, individuals may feel empowered to abuse their authority without fear of consequences. This can be exacerbated by poor governance, weak oversight or a culture that tolerates or rewards aggressive behaviour.

- *Toxic work cultures:* In organisations that emphasise competition, power and control over collaboration and ethics, individuals may feel pressured to abuse power as a means of survival or advancement.

A lack of clear structures and systems to manage the flow of power leads to corrupt cultures and toxic norms. But it is fixable. I get to that in chapter 14, where I discuss building positive power structures.

---

[9] This study concurs with Dr Kelther's findings: Gruenfeld, D, et al (2008), 'Power and the objectification of social targets', *Journal of Personality and Social Psychology*, June, www.researchgate.net/publication/5246875_Power_and_the_Objectification_of_Social_Targets.

Cultural or organisational norms

The norms we adhere to can also allow the abuse of power to continue:

- *Normalisation of power abuse:* In some organisations or societies, abuse of power is normalised or even encouraged as part of the organisational culture. Employees may learn these behaviours by observing higher-ups engaging in manipulative tactics, leading to a cycle of abuse.

- *Social expectations:* In some cases, cultural or societal expectations (for example, traditional views on leadership, gender roles or hierarchy) may drive individuals to behave in ways that maintain their power, even if it means engaging in unethical practices.

Again, if sound structures and effective systems are not in place, these cultural norms can become embedded pretty quickly. It just takes one leader not to say something when they observe poor behaviour for it to take root as normal. And if it's the leader who is doling out the abuse, it's even worse. Pick your favourite scandal and see how these kinds of norms have taken root in environments such as religious institutions, military services and schools.

Greed and ambition

I know you were waiting for this one! Here's how good old greed and ambition can play into the abuse of power:

- *Personal gain:* Some people abuse power to gain wealth, status or other forms of personal advancement. The pursuit of personal ambition, coupled with the ability to manipulate or control others, can lead to corrupt practices such as financial exploitation or unethical decision-making.

- *Desire for status:* The desire to climb the social or corporate ladder can drive individuals to use their power ruthlessly to outmanoeuvre rivals and secure their own position.

Greed and ambition are the easiest rationale for the arseholery we see in destructive Power Games. But as I've just outlined, and will expand on in the chapters on archetypes and their shadows in part III, they're not the only reasons.

If you are to combat Power Games, you need to know a little more about them. Let's dive in.

POWER GAMES BEGIN

Serena stormed from the room, down the corridor and into a private office where she flung herself into a chair.

Damn him! He is such a dickhead, she thought.

Her colleague Devon had stolen her design idea and pitched it to their boss, claiming it as his own. The audacity! She'd overheard Devon bragging about the design idea to some of the other world designers. Now he was in line for the promotion she longed for.

And if she said anything to their boss, Dan, it would look like sour grapes.

Serena drummed her fingers on the table, scowling. *It just goes to show you can't trust anyone. He was supposed to be my friend! Office politics suck.*

She sat back in the chair, rubbing her hands together, thinking.

If she was going to be sidelined and undermined in this company, she wouldn't take it lying down. Gaia Enterprises had just issued a call out for world designers on the Olympus Project, the first long-term habitable moonbase, and Serena would make sure she was the nominated candidate from their company. She was sure Devon was eyeing that opportunity, too. They all were.

Devon, that smug bastard, thought he was the front-runner.

Not so fast, you slimy toad, she thought and smiled to herself.

Devon was having an affair with Dan's wife. As Devon's friend, she had raised an eyebrow and shook her head, but kept quiet. It was his business and life to screw up. But now he had stolen credit for her ideas. The gloves were off.

You screwed with me, Devon, and now there's hell to pay.

CHAPTER 2

UNDERSTANDING POWER GAMES

When I ran a survey of leaders around Australia, I discovered this astonishing fact: 100 per cent of respondents had experienced Power Games in the workplace. These ranged from the mildly irritating to the serious and traumatising, including things such as credit stealing and blame shifting, all the way through to gaslighting and undermining.

Power Games occur across the spectrum of roles and levels within an organisation. However, authority and position can determine the extent and nature of the negative deployment of power.

In this chapter, I cover the kinds of Power Games that can come from those in charge, as well as those played between colleagues.

Power at the top

When it comes to Power Games, the more insidious versions come from the top – that is, from people with formal authority.

Bosses can engage in various office politics or Power Games to maintain control, manipulate team dynamics or protect their authority. Here are some common tactics.

Favouritism, nepotism and exclusion

Bosses might grant promotions, praise or opportunities disproportionately to certain individuals (often based on loyalty, not merit). When this is directed towards friends or family, it becomes nepotism. In these situations, a manager promotes or provides special treatment to friends or family members regardless of merit, denying others fair opportunities for advancement.

Who can forget Trump's employment tactics during his first Presidency in the White House? Family members were non-elected advisors. He demanded 'absolute loyalty' from staffers in his term as President. Those who failed the loyalty test were quickly ousted – including the head of the FBI, James Comey. As I write this, Trump has been elected to the White House once more. Let's see what Power Games emerge in his second bite at the cherry.

If certain employees are not part of the 'in' crowd, bosses may exclude these employees from important meetings or decisions, undermining their influence and visibility within the organisation. And this is more prevalent than you might think – according to a survey from online job search site Monster, 72 per cent of workers have witnessed favouritism from a manager.[10]

Divide and conquer

This tactic involves pitting team members against each other or fostering competition between employees to prevent them from uniting and challenging the boss's authority.

By creating divisions, the boss maintains control and avoids facing a united group. This is something Rupert Murdoch failed to do well. He positioned his eldest son as the heir-apparent to the family business, Fox Corporation. The countermove from three other siblings was to band together to challenge the change in the family trust's arrangements. In this case, power came in uniting, not dividing.

Micromanagement

A boss may micromanage employees to assert dominance, often undermining their autonomy and trust. This makes employees overly dependent on the boss for approval or direction.

---

10 Monster (2023) 'Poll results: Workplace red flags', Monster, August, learnmore.monster.com/workplace-red-flags-poll-results.

This is one of the more common complaints about bad bosses and it is crippling to a worker's confidence and wellbeing. According to the Monster survey, 73 per cent of workers consider micro-management the biggest workplace 'red flag', and 46 per cent identify it as a reason they would leave their job.[11]

Information withholding

Some bosses retain critical information to maintain an upper hand in decision-making, making employees less informed and less able to act independently. Knowledge is power in this case.

Credit stealing

A common power game is where bosses take credit for the ideas or hard work of their team members, diminishing others' visibility and claiming sole recognition for success.

According to BambooHR's Bad Boss survey, employees rate credit stealing as the worst thing bosses can do.[12] It just stinks of pettiness and selfishness.

Sabotage

A manipulative boss might subtly sabotage an employee's project – or even career – by withholding resources, delaying decisions or providing poor guidance, ensuring the employee fails to meet expectations. This kind of boss must have some serious issues with you if this happening. Likely, they see you as some sort of threat.

Blame shifting

When things go wrong, some bosses shift blame onto subordinates to protect their own position and reputation, regardless of who is truly at fault. Dastardly fiends!

---

11 Ibid.
12 Guest blogger (2019), 'Bad Boss Index: 1,000 employees name worst manager behaviors', BambooHR blog, 19 March, www.bamboohr.com/blog/bad-boss-index-the-worst-boss-behaviors-according-to-employees-infographic.

Controlling communication

Bosses might control the flow of communication by acting as the sole conduit between higher management and employees, thereby controlling the narrative and what gets passed on. This makes it difficult for counter moves because they manage the narrative – they're not impossible, but hard.

Gaslighting

In more toxic environments, a boss may engage in gaslighting, making employees question their own judgement, decisions or recollection of events, and thereby undermining their confidence and independence. This is how toxic bosses keep people scared and dancing like puppets.

Promoting incompetence

Some bosses will promote individuals who are less competent or less threatening than other employees to avoid challenges to their authority. This also makes the promoted individuals dependent on the boss. They don't want to be upstaged by any of their team members. Ugh.

Selective enforcement of rules

A boss may enforce rules unevenly, giving some employees more leniency while holding others to stricter standards, fostering a culture of fear and uncertainty. This screams of unfairness and is a good segue for bitterness.

Playing the victim

In some cases, bosses may portray themselves as the victim of circumstances or disloyal employees, deflecting criticism and gaining sympathy to maintain control. This technique can backfire when a savvy board holds the weasel boss to account.

Over-promising and under-delivering

A boss might promise raises, promotions or new opportunities to keep employees motivated but never follow through, using these promises to maintain loyalty without providing real benefits. What a jerk!

If reading this list made you sweat at the sheer douchebaggery potential of bad actors in positions of authority, you are not alone. Worse, you may have experienced some of these practices yourself. If so, my deep condolences to you and congratulations on surviving such horrendous conditions.

Unfortunately, the bad behaviour can get worse.

TALES FROM THE TRENCHES

Consider these examples of bosses abusing their power.

Left out in the cold

After a thirty-year career, I found myself on the outer. I had always been fiercely independent, reliable and trusted by my bosses. I got the job done. My clients liked my work. Then my boss started micromanaging me. I couldn't understand it. Then I worked out the new secretary was turning her against me. I realised my boss had developed a huge dependency on the secretary, who was now the only filter to my boss, and the only one she would listen to. All of a sudden, I was being 'performance managed', told there were complaints from 'lots of people', and that I was not to contact any of my clients directly. They wouldn't give me any evidence or offer any due process. I felt so betrayed. I lost trust in people, went on sick leave and eventually left.

Sucking up and manipulation by others can lead to ostracisation, isolation and loss of employment. The sense of betrayal after being a dedicated, loyal worker can be debilitating. Indeed, it took this individual months of therapy before being able to consider working again.

She said she wanted honest feedback

I had always had a good rapport with my CEO. She was well-loved and appreciated. Then she resigned, a new CEO joined and things went weird. The new CEO was a bit of a train wreck. She was domineering in meetings and squashed innovation. I had always been encouraged by the previous CEO to share my opinions, especially if it was for the good of the organisation. I was confident in my observations but nervous about sharing them, but I did so anyway. The new CEO said she wanted honest feedback, so I gave her my thoughts on how things were going and what she might consider doing differently. Well, she didn't like that at all. She started sidelining me. I wasn't given any new projects and was taken off my favourite committee. There were closed-door conversations I wasn't invited to. I lost autonomy and had to run every single thing past her. So much for speaking the truth.

Being encouraged to be assertive and speak up is sound advice from a supportive leader. But when the people change and the system doesn't, Power Games like undermining to shore up the leader's own status can emerge.

Spurned suitor

When I was working in a bar paying my way through university, the head waiter thought I was having an affair with the restaurant owner. He must have thought

I was an easy target or something because he suggested a threesome with me and one of the other wait staff. I turned him down, completely shocked. Realising he had gotten it totally wrong, he started making life difficult for me. He followed me around, especially when the owner was on site, to make sure I didn't pass on what had happened. Then he scheduled me on all the crappy shifts, including double ones. He yelled at me in front of other staff, and because the night shift bar manager was his friend, I got no help at the end of the night cleaning up my section. After weeks of working crazy hours and feeling like a punching bag, I finally quit, stressed out and exhausted.

Positional authority can lead to impulsive, inappropriate behaviour. When those individuals get called out, survival mechanisms kick in and oppressive and domineering behaviour can emerge from those who stand to lose their status.

What can we conclude from these observations? Working with others can be hazardous for your health.

Abuse and misuse of power

Abuse of power occurs when individuals in positions of authority misuse their authority for personal gain, to manipulate or to harm others.

Buckle up – we're heading into some pretty nasty territory.

Bullying and intimidation

This is the use of positional power to instil fear rather than manage fairly. A boss might threaten employees with termination or punitive measures to ensure compliance or submission, even when such actions are unjustified. I had a client, a CEO, who reported these types of threats after every meeting with the Chair. He would issue veiled threats of terminating her position if she did not deliver the report/strategy/outcome he expected. She lived in constant anticipation of losing her job and her work became harder than ever, with overwhelming anxiety.

Sexual harassment

A boss can exploit their authority to coerce, intimidate or manipulate employees into unwanted situations. A supervisor, for example, might use their position to make inappropriate sexual advances towards employees, with the implication that rejection may result in career repercussions.

Been there? If the #MeToo movement showed us anything, it's how widespread this issue is.

Financial exploitation

The power-hungry, deluded leader might misappropriate company assets for personal enrichment – in other words, steal.

This can include using company funds or resources for personal use without consent, such as expensing lavish vacations or personal items. It might even extend to unauthorised 'loans'. Surprisingly, remorse for this kind of 'lending' is low, with the perpetrators often feeling justified in their actions because they always intended to pay it back. Really.

Manipulation of metrics and performance

Abuse of power can get pretty personal and twisted. Some bosses might alter performance evaluations for personal motives, such as settling old scores or maintaining control. They might manipulate performance reviews or key performance indicators (KPIs) to make certain employees look bad, either to justify firing them or preventing their promotion.

Grudges, anyone?

Discriminatory practices

Sometimes a boss may not be aware of their discrimination. We all have cognitive biases. When this discrimination is deliberate, however, it's next level heinous: misusing authority to marginalise individuals or groups based on biases, rather than job performance or qualifications. This might look like an executive who enforces discriminatory hiring or promotion, or has disciplinary practices based on race, gender or other protected characteristics.

Yeah, this shit still happens.

Coercion and blackmail

Unfortunately, coercion and blackmail is not just the purview of gritty political thrillers like *House of Cards*. Bad bosses might force employees into compromising positions under the threat of punitive actions. How about this one: a supervisor coerces an employee into unethical behaviour (for example, falsifying reports) by threatening job loss or negative professional repercussions if they refuse.

***

Well, I'm not sure about you, but that list makes me yearn for a stiff drink.

Can the workplace really be the purview of such manipulative and caustic behaviour? Unfortunately, yes. But we do have solutions.

Before we brazen through to next steps in our quest to inoculate against scandalous power-mongering, let's not forget the Power Games that can occur between colleagues. So swig that gin and tonic (or beverage of choice), and let's take a look at Power Games between team members.

Power Games between colleagues

If you don't have a manipulative boss, hoorah! But you may have to contend with Power Games between peers. Here are some tactics they might use.

Building alliances and coalitions

Creating informal networks with colleagues is a powerful tool. Employees can build relationships with influential peers, higher-ups or even clients to gain leverage and influence without having formal authority.

Ganging up against a supervisor can be a useful power move if that supervisor is a tyrant. A collective can help protect the group from unfavourable decisions or to resist authority.

Forming a gang or coalition to sideline colleagues is less cool. But it happens. Schoolyard shenanigans can resurface at work.

Gossip and rumour spreading

Employees might engage in gossip or spread rumours to manipulate perceptions of others or to undermine rivals in the workplace. This kind of behaviour is often aimed at damaging the reputation of others to elevate their own standing.

Strategic leaking of information can be used to influence decisions or outcomes in subtle ways. Rumours of family troubles, a mysterious illness or illicit love affair can tarnish a person's image by subtly implying that the person is somehow 'less than' with these issues. Insidious.

Passive resistance

Employees can use passive resistance – for example, intentionally working slow, avoiding tasks or subtly resisting initiatives they don't agree with – to influence outcomes. This is a non-confrontational way to express dissent without direct confrontation.

In *People Stuff*, I called this brand of passive-aggressiveness the purview of the Ground Splitter: someone who resists by undermining.

Flattery and manipulation

Ahh, the good ole suck-up! Flattering superiors is a common tactic employees use to gain favour and advance without necessarily earning it through merit.

Then you have the 'woe is me' buttercup. These employees manipulate emotions by making themselves appear indispensable or overworked, subtly playing on the boss's sympathy or concern.

Credit claiming and deflecting blame

Some people never grow out of freeloader tactics such as claiming credit on projects they did little work on. (This may bring back horrible memories of university group projects where some just coasted on the efforts of others. *Shudder*.) More sophisticated manipulation comes when your astute shirker positions themselves strategically in front of management when the time comes for recognition.

And then these same people are also usually quick to deflect blame for mistakes onto others, a survival tactic that helps them maintain a positive image while avoiding responsibility for failure.

If you're currently carrying the dead weight of these nasty creatures, I feel for you.

Hoarding information

At earlier stages of leadership maturity, we might enjoy feeling like the smartest person in the room, steeped in specialist expertise. Then most of us work out that maybe other smart people are around us too. In this situation, those who play Power Games might start to withhold critical information or resources to maintain control and power over a situation. This can make them seem more indispensable as the go-to person for specific knowledge or data.

If that's you, stop it! That's playing for a team of one and it's in the shadow side of Power Games.

Undermining colleagues

Undermining others through subtle sabotage (such as withholding support, giving misleading advice or setting unrealistic expectations) is a way to weaken a colleague's standing and make them appear less competent.

One leader I worked with mentioned a staff member who would drop subtle undermining bombs like this: 'It's not really Esmerelda's fault. She's not really up to the job and is a bit out of her depth'.

This is so manipulative! It's appearing to be empathetic while gouging the person's competence in front of the boss. Gag.

Playing the victim

Employees might play the victim card, painting themselves as unfairly treated or as martyrs to elicit sympathy from management or co-workers. This tactic can shift attention away from performance issues and onto perceived injustices.

We can all get hooked by this 'drama triangle'[13] ploy. Resist the temptation to rush in and save the day.

Strategic volunteering

Volunteering for high-visibility projects is a way for employees to increase their exposure to senior leaders and gain recognition. Even if they don't have formal power, being associated with successful initiatives boosts their reputation.

While not overtly evil, this tactic can turn dark if the person sharpens their elbows to nudge other contenders out of the running (perhaps using some of the tactics just discussed).

---

13 Stephen Karpman's drama triangle is an insightful model that maps the destructive dynamics of people in conflict. It's bad. Stay out of it. Read more here: Wikipedia, 'Karpman drama triangle', en.wikipedia.org/wiki/Karpman_drama_triangle.

Timing and visibility

This is an adjunct to the suck-up. Being strategically visible at the right time (for example, staying late when the boss is around or delivering work right before a meeting) can give the impression of dedication and hard work, even if it's not consistent with the employee's actual output.

Delaying information or tasks strategically to force decisions in their favour is another tactic that gives employees some control. Admittedly, this takes some cunning and foresight. If only they used these smarts for good.

Feigning incompetence

Feigning incompetence at tasks they don't want to do can be a way for employees to avoid work or push undesirable tasks onto others, while focusing on more favourable projects.

I admit it. For a long time I pretended not to know how to cook, so my husband took up that duty, and I enjoyed years of home-cooked meals free of my personal effort. When my diet changed due to a coeliac diagnosis, I was forced to experiment with new recipes and my cover was blown. My husband was amazed. And now I share the cooking. Sigh.

While these employee tactics are often covert, they can significantly impact office dynamics. Employees who don't have formal power may use these strategies to influence outcomes, protect their position or advance their careers. However, these tactics can also contribute to a toxic work environment if not managed properly. Lack of structures and processes can allow these types of peer power plays to run rampant.

Worse, if a peer who uses these tactics actually gets rewarded and promoted, they then have positional authority to wield even greater Power Games.

Comparing the Power Games of bosses and peers

Let's take a look at the similarities and differences between the ways these Power Games can be used by bosses and peers, starting with the similarities.

Similarities between bosses and peers

Here's how bosses and peers can use similar tactics when playing with power:

- *Information withholding:*
  - Bosses may withhold critical information to maintain control, keeping employees dependent on them.
  - Employees can also withhold information or skills to make themselves appear indispensable or to undermine colleagues.
  - Both use information control to manipulate outcomes and create a power imbalance.

- *Favouritism and alliance building:*
  - Bosses can promote or favour certain employees to maintain loyalty, creating divisions within teams.
  - Employees often build alliances or coalitions to protect themselves, gain influence or challenge authority.
  - Both sides use personal relationships to bolster their power or position within the organisation.

- *Credit claiming:*
  - Bosses might take credit for the work of their team to appear more competent or influential.
  - Employees can also claim credit for successful projects to gain recognition from peers or superiors.
  - Both seek recognition as a form of power, often at the expense of others.

- *Undermining others:*
  - Bosses may undermine employees by withholding support or setting unrealistic expectations to ensure their failure.
  - Employees can subtly sabotage colleagues by offering misleading advice or withholding help.
  - Both engage in undermining to maintain or advance their standing, often in covert ways.

Differences between bosses and peers

Bosses and peers may use and abuse power differently, including in the following ways:

- *Positional power:*
  - Bosses have legitimate authority and control over resources such as promotions, raises or job security, which they can use as tools in Power Games (for example, through reward or coercive power).
  - Employees without formal authority must rely on influence tactics such as alliances, persuasion or manipulation.
  - Bosses have direct control over formal rewards and punishments, while employees must be more creative in gaining leverage through social influence.
- *Blame-shifting:*
  - Bosses can shift blame onto subordinates to protect their own position when things go wrong.
  - Employees often blame colleagues or external factors to avoid accountability.
  - A boss's blame-shifting can have greater consequences, such as disciplinary actions against employees, whereas an employee's blame game is often about self-preservation within the team.

- *Micromanagement versus passive resistance:*
  - Bosses use micromanagement as a control tactic, asserting dominance by closely monitoring and controlling how work is done.
  - Employees without formal control often use passive resistance (for example, working slowly or avoiding tasks) as a way to undermine authority.
  - Bosses micromanage to assert overt control, while employees use subtle resistance to challenge that control without direct confrontation.
- *Flattery versus favouritism:*
  - Bosses show favouritism to certain employees, using promotions or benefits as rewards for loyalty.
  - Employees engage in flattery and ingratiation to curry favour with their boss, hoping to receive special treatment.
  - Bosses use favouritism as a tool to manage loyalty and control, while employees flatter to secure opportunities and climb the ladder.

While both bosses and employees engage in similar Power Games, such as information withholding, alliance-building and blame-shifting, the key difference lies in their access to resources and authority. Bosses wield formal power and can control career outcomes directly, while employees rely on social influence, alliances and subtle tactics to gain leverage in the workplace.

After this exploration of the Power Games horror show, I think I need a shower. But the burning question is *why?* Why do people behave so atrociously?

So go to the sink, splash your face, and let's figure this out.

Looking at what's really behind power games

In my conversations with leaders, I've often asked what they thought was at the root of the power problem. Some felt that the power players were ego maniacs, hell-bent on advancing their own career and claiming as many accolades for themselves as possible. Others felt the Power Games were due to personality conflicts – putting them down to just very different people in the workplace having clashes and creating problems. And some leaders felt that in certain situations a power grab occurred so that certain people could dictate the group's direction and approach. Their campaign of 'my way will be the only highway' drove the office politics.

Some of these factors may contribute in some way to the Power Games we all experience to a certain extent, but my research has found that other, more solvable, issues contribute more significantly.

What the problem is *not*

Let's look first at what my research has shown aren't major factors in Power Games.

The problem is not trust

Good collaboration can still occur where trust is absent. It's not a necessary prerequisite. If you have an industry association that needs to bring together stakeholders with competing priorities, for example, trust is not necessarily required for a good working effort around the table.

Trust, however, is a by-product of good structure in a team environment. This structure includes agreed ways of working, decision-making protocols and accountability for commitments. I address the detail of what good structure is in chapter 14.

The problem is not culture

Culture is not the *cause* of Power Games. Good culture is the *effect* of good systems. So if an organisation has a culture problem, it's a symptom, alongside Power Games, as opposed to the cause. If we focus on developing good systems within organisations, we can alleviate many of the symptoms that come with poor systems.

These good systems include recruitment, recognition, reward and promotion.

With good systems comes good culture. With good systems, the abuse of power is harder to hide. Good systems quickly expose the weed of power problems, and we can then rip them up at the roots.

What's the real problem that drives Power Games?

My research has shown that the factors that contribute most strongly to Power Games in the workplace include the following:

- *The leadership maturity of the players:* Each of us comes with a set of values and motivations, and these may set us as opponents to our colleagues if we are not aware or transparent about them.

- *A lack of language or protocol to talk about power:* Power is a bugaboo that irks many. Ask anyone if they want more power and they shiver in repulsion. Ask them if they want more influence and, all of a sudden, hands go up. We want power and influence; we just don't want to fall prey to its traps.

- *No systems in place to address power struggles:* Working with others is one of life's greatest joys – and one of its biggest pains. No-one likes office politics and many of us like to think we are above them. But we all have an agenda. We all want to make a difference and, sometimes, that creates power struggles. Without systems to harness these good intentions of purposeful contribution, things can quickly get ugly.

- *No structures to prevent Power Games:* Even in flat hierarchies with few positions of formal power, we need structure. Prevention of Power Games requires transparent and useful structures to manage the flow of resources and privileges.

- *Low self-awareness of how to wield power without becoming a tyrant:* All of us carry shadows within our altruistic archetypes. Savvy leaders mind their shadow and avoid the temptations that draw them into destructive Power Games. I discuss these archetypes – and their shadows – in much more detail in part III.

Now you have a better idea of what Power Games are, let's delve into how power manifests itself in the Four Spheres of Power.

PART II

DEVELOPING THE FOUR SPHERES OF POWER

What are the magic ingredients that make up our capacity to get stuff done across different contexts? Allow me to introduce the Four Spheres of Power.

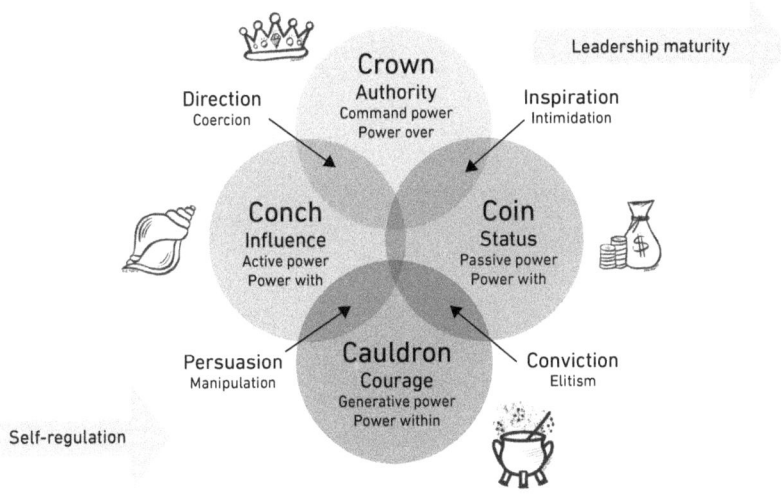

You can combine elements from each of these four spheres to build your leadership power and use your influence for good. The chapters in this part take you through how to do this.

CHAPTER 3

INTRODUCING THE FOUR SPHERES OF POWER

In this chapter, I provide a quick overview of the four spheres and how they interconnect. In the following four chapters, I run through each of the spheres in more detail.

Cauldron: Courage

At the bottom of the Four Spheres of Power model, we have the Cauldron of Courage. This is generative power, and solely within your own control; hence, it is power 'within'. You can build up the steam and heat coming from your cauldron by honing your beliefs, self-talk and sense of agency. Courageous actions build your self-esteem and help you exercise power in your immediate personal world, before you start to exercise influence with others. This cauldron is your source of strength in all three of the other spheres. Feeling powerless? Start here. I dive into the nitty-gritty of this sphere in the next chapter.

Coin: Status

The next sphere, Coin, represents status – a power 'with', but a passive form of power that can be earned or unearned. Unearned status can be conferred on an individual by virtue of their innate traits or social position. This, of course, is what we refer to as 'privilege'.

For example, cultural background and gender might earn more status points in different contexts. Being 'white' and 'male' is usually considered to provide – unearned – lottery-sized status points.

Earned status can include reputation, expertise, experience, achievements, credibility, wealth and resource control, visibility and public recognition through things such as public speaking, media appearances or social media presence.

Employees who possess specialised knowledge or skills that are valuable to the organisation often gain informal power. These 'knowledge brokers' are frequently sought out by colleagues and leaders for advice or guidance, making them key players in decision-making processes. Their expertise gives them leverage, even if they don't hold formal leadership positions.

An example of this could be an IT expert in a tech company. Through knowing the intricacies of a critical system, this employee might be consulted regularly, giving them the ability to shape how projects are executed, even if they aren't officially in charge of the project.

The symbol of the Coin represents social currency, accumulated privilege and passive influence. This 'Coin' is what you possess due to your position, connections, wealth or history, rather than direct action.

Key aspects of status

The key aspects of status and the Coin sphere include the following:

- *Accumulation:* Status builds over time – you can collect 'Coin' (such as privileges, titles and recognition) through achievements, networks and social positioning.
- *Privilege:* With status comes certain privileges – including access, respect and a platform that others might not have.
- *Perception by others:* Status is more about how others see you, giving you influence by association or by position.

- *Passive force:* You influence passively – by existing within a certain echelon, being perceived as important, and thus being deferred to or admired.

The Coin is influence that comes from the accumulation of privilege or social positioning, rather than direct action. It is power through status or standing, rather than actively swaying others through speech or visibility.

Conch: Influence

The Conch sphere represents influence – that is, the ability to shape behaviours or decisions through relationships, expertise or persuasion. Influence is more informal and subtle than authority or control, but can sometimes be more pervasive and effective. It operates without formal or positional power, relying on persuasion, relationships, charisma and social capital. Influence is an active form of power, a power 'with' others. People who wield influence often do so through networks, reputation and personal relationships.

The symbol of the Conch represents the ability to use your voice to sway others. It's a symbol of active influence, where you speak up, take centre stage and command attention through your words, ideas or presence.

Key aspect of influence

Influence and the Conch have the following key aspects:

- *Charisma:* The power of personality, being compelling and persuasive.

- *Visibility:* Being seen and heard, leading others through communication.

- *Impact on others:* Influence can be immediate – when you use your voice, your influence can cause a direct shift in opinion, action or behaviour.

- *Dynamic force:* Influence is through leadership, persuasion and the use of communication.

The Conch sphere focuses on how influence is expressed, particularly through speech and visibility. It's about being in the spotlight and steering the conversation or decisions. Conch influence can take other forms, however. These include:

- *Influence through relationships:* Informal networks are built on personal and professional relationships that develop outside of the formal chain of command. Employees with strong interpersonal connections across different departments or levels of the organisation can wield significant influence by facilitating communication, solving problems or advocating for ideas. These individuals often act as connectors, sharing information and insights that might not flow through formal channels.

  An example of this is an employee who has built close relationships with both senior leaders and peers. They then may have the ability to shape decisions by knowing who to talk to, what information to share and how to influence outcomes, without holding formal authority.

- *Influence through social capital and trust:* Social capital refers to the trust and goodwill that individuals accumulate through positive interactions, collaboration and networking. Employees with high social capital can navigate the organisation more effectively and influence others by leveraging their reputation for trustworthiness, competence and cooperation. This informal power can be especially effective in times of crisis or change when people look to those they trust for guidance.

  An example here is a well-respected mid-level employee who might be able to rally support for a new initiative or project because they have built a strong reputation for reliability and competence among colleagues across the organisation.

A NOTE ON PASSIVE AND ACTIVE POWER

Informal power networks can be considered *active* power when individuals in these networks deliberately use their influence to achieve specific goals. For instance, someone might leverage their relationships to advocate for a project, push through an initiative or sway a decision in a meeting. In this case, the individual is actively engaging their social connections to exert influence.

Another example is a well-networked employee who rallies support for a new initiative by having conversations with key stakeholders. This person is using active social power to shape the outcome – and so is using the Conch.

Informal networks can also exhibit *passive* power when influence is wielded indirectly or without deliberate intention. In these situations, a person's influence comes from their reputation or status within the network, even if they are not actively pushing an agenda. Others may defer to them or seek their input simply because they trust their judgment or expertise.

For example, a long-serving employee who has a reputation for being knowledgeable may passively influence decisions, even when they are not directly involved in discussions. Their opinion carries weight, and decisions may be shaped by their unspoken influence. This is how you leverage Coin.

How status (Coin) and influence (Conch) relate

Status and influence are interconnected. If you have status (Coin), you naturally hold a level of influence (Conch). The more status you accumulate, the more social credibility you gain, which in turn amplifies your voice and increases your ability to influence.

However:

- *Conch = direct:* The Conch represents active influence – you're using your voice and presence to lead, persuade and impact.

- *Coin = indirect:* The Coin represents indirect influence, where your mere presence, title or accumulated privilege grants you influence without you needing to say anything. You're given a seat at the table because of your status, and others may follow your lead by default.

Other distinctions include the following:

- Volatility:
  - *Conch:* Influence through charisma and voice can be fleeting – today's leader can lose influence if they fall out of favour or stop using their voice effectively.
  - *Coin:* Status, once accumulated, is harder to lose – it's more enduring. Even if you fall from the spotlight, the privilege and accumulated 'wealth' of your status often remain.

- Source of power:
  - *Conch:* Influence via the Conch comes from skill, presence and ability to engage.
  - *Coin:* Status comes from wealth, connections, history or achievements that others recognise.

- Who benefits:
  - *Conch:* Others benefit from your direct leadership and guidance – you're actively shaping outcomes.
  - *Coin:* Others may defer to you without you needing to act, because they perceive your status and position as trustworthy or prestigious.

The Coin and Conch spheres overlap and work together, but one is about active leadership and the other is about positional advantage.

Crown: Authority

Finally, at the top of the four spheres model, we have authority. This is what most people typically think of when it comes to power. Authority is the power of command, of power 'over' others, and is hierarchical in nature. And it's where the susceptibility to abuse and corruption is most likely to rear its ugly head.

Authority is the formal right to make decisions based on a position or role. Authority usually comes with certain controls, such as the ability to direct resources, processes or outcomes.

While power is the ability to influence or control the behaviour of people, authority is the recognised and accepted use of power. Authority implies a certain level of voluntary compliance from those subject to it, distinguishing it from mere coercion or force.

Key aspects of authority

Authority is recognised as *legitimate* power. This legitimacy can be derived from laws, rules, norms or social acceptance. Max Weber, a prominent sociologist, identified three types of legitimate authority:

- *Traditional authority:* Derived from long-established customs, traditions or social structures (for example, monarchies).

- *Charismatic authority:* Based on the personal charm or leadership qualities of an individual (for example, leaders such as Martin Luther King Jr or Mahatma Gandhi).

- *Rational–legal authority:* Rooted in established laws, procedures and institutions (for example, elected officials, bureaucracies).

In addition, the following types of authority also exist:

- *Organisational authority:* Within organisations, authority is often structured hierarchically, with defined roles and responsibilities (for example, managers and executives). This type of authority ensures order and efficiency in operations.

- *Political authority:* In the context of governance, political authority refers to the power held by individuals or institutions to create and enforce laws, policies and decisions (for example, governments and law enforcement agencies).

- *Moral authority:* This type of authority is based on ethical or moral grounds, where individuals or groups are respected and followed due to their perceived integrity and moral standards (for example, religious leaders and activists).

Challenges to authority

Authority can be challenged or undermined through various means, such as social movements, revolutions, or changes in societal values and norms. The legitimacy of authority is crucial; when it is perceived as unjust or ineffective, it can lead to resistance or upheaval.

The Crown is the obvious symbol of this sphere of power: the Crown is won, stolen or awarded, and marks supremacy or rule with a long history across cultures.

Power pathways

At the intersection of these spheres are different power pathways, as follows:

- *Persuasion:* With courage (Cauldron) and influence (Conch), you can persuade others to change beliefs or take action.

- *Conviction:* With courage (Cauldron) and status (Coin), you develop conviction. While a passive form of power, conviction can be compelling – after all, few things are more attractive than confidence born of conviction. Who doesn't love a passionate figure dedicated to a cause?

- *Inspiration:* With status (Coin) and authority (Crown), you have the potential for inspiration. Someone with plenty of Coins in their status bag, combined with a Crown of formal authority, can wield tremendous inspiration. A leader who has 'worked their way up the ladder', with enormous respect, expertise and experience, who achieves formal authority, demonstrates how power and command can be earned with diligence and hard work, inspiring others.

- *Direction:* Ah, the heady combination of authority (Crown) and influence (Conch). This is a leader who has both formal control and personal persuasion to set a path, galvanise the troops and step to it.

Power pitfalls

You may have noticed that the intersecting pathways on the Four Spheres of Power model also harbour power traps. Direction can become coercion, inspiration can quickly turn to intimidation, persuasion to manipulation, and conviction to dogmatism. I explore more of these power traps when I look at the archetypes and their shadows in part III, including how to avoid stumbling unwittingly into these ethical pits of power hell.

For now, it is important to note that framing the Four Spheres of Power are two dimensions that affect the deployment of power: leadership maturity and self-regulation.

Self-regulation is your ability to self-observe, monitor and manage your thoughts and emotions, and take considered action. The better your self-regulation, the better you can steer your ship of power. Self-regulation is also your best bet in reining in any tiptoeing towards power pitfalls. Poor self-regulation sets you up for all sorts of stumbles, from power abuse through to losing power.

Leadership maturity determines the sphere and scope of your use of power, and how you perceive its benefits. Leadership maturity is a developmental model that argues adults continue to develop in stages when it comes to ego (sense of self) and action logic (how we see and act in the world).

These stages are as follows:
- Diplomat
- Expert
- Achiever
- Individualist
- Strategist.

At earlier stages of leadership maturity, such as during the Diplomat stage of ego development, our exercise of power is strictly to ensure we maintain social norms and bonds and secure our position within the group. If we grow through the stages, we can develop an ever more inclusive sense of our place in the world, navigate complexity better, and manage more intractable, complex challenges.[14]

Let's walk through the stages to see what you are up against, both in terms of your own leadership maturity and that of the others playing Power Games with you.

Diplomat

During this stage, our focus is on fitting in, obeying and supporting social norms and law. Our sense of safety and ego comes from belonging, of being part of a group. We avoid anything that might put us outside of the group or challenge the group's norms, be they good or evil. From a power point of view, we are unlikely to speak up about abuses of power, even if we know them to be wrong, because this would challenge the overall safety of our tribe. This is how we might become complicit in Power Games that defy our personal values. In terms of exercising power, we might use our influence to resist threats to the group, its norms and rules, and back the leader(s). This is where groupthink can take root.

---

14 For more information, please see Susanne Cook-Greuter's work on ego development and leadership maturity, available via instituteofcoaching.org/author/cook-greuter-susanne, and Bill Torbert's work in action inquiry, at www.williamrtorbert.com/action-inquiry/.

Expert

At this stage, we work out that our experience and expertise are of value, and we start to exercise our voice, sometimes in conflict with the leader's point of view or the group's default perspective. This can be a challenging time, and radically different to the Diplomat stage as we seek to stand out, not fit in. We rely on the expertise and credentials in our Coin bag to wield influence and amplify our Conch.

The challenge from a power point of view is that we can be judgemental of others who do not live up to our credibility standards, and we may also be single-minded in our perspective. We see through the lens of our expertise and may find it challenging to see others' points of view, thereby limiting our ability to collaborate and execute on collective projects. In other words, we might think we are challenging 'wrong thinking' when in fact we might simply be an obstacle to change. If we gain a position with formal authority at this stage, the risk for us is task hoarding, poor delegation and micromanaging. As Experts, we often feel that no-one else has enough experience or know-how to do things as well as us, so we become a 'my way or the highway' type of leader. Yikes.

Achiever

As we grow in responsibility, we develop the realisation that working with others can yield greater results. We can't rely on our Coin solely to accomplish everything, and so develop our ability to delegate, coordinate and collaborate. A dose of humility and courage amplifies our Conch here. This stage is often when we achieve a position of authority and work with a Crown in an official capacity.

Our challenge at Achiever stage is trying to do too much – if we fire our Cauldron up high, we risk burning our natural courage and energy into crusty, smoking remnants. Our ability to influence is diminished by our exhaustion, as is our ability to navigate complexity, share workloads and see beyond the immediate horizon.

Individualist

This stage marks a huge shift in perspective. We embrace the gifts of diversity, are curious about people's experiences and backgrounds, and seek out novelty. We are hungry to see things from multiple angles, and revel in exploring complexity through systems thinking. For a power point of view, we may become more adept at using our Conch, and tackle use of our Crown from an inclusive, egalitarian way.

The danger for us here is taking too much time and effort to make decisions. We might also have our compassion dialled up high and so be reluctant to use our courage to take action for things like discipline, believing the best in others. From a power point of view, Power Games might emerge if we do not hold the reins tight enough on our team, as they vie for influence in a more fluid team arrangement.

Strategist

If we grow out of the challenges of the Individualist stage, we manage to balance the need for compassionate consultation with effective, big-picture thinking. We are able to work with a long-term horizon, and manage the nimble requirements of the present moment. Sounds terrific, right?

The power trap for us here is that we may have dialled up our wisdom too high and become a little dispassionate towards the issues and challenges confronting the team today. We lose a bit of our Conch as we rely more on our intellectual grunt in our Coin bag. Undercurrents of discontent and resistance may arise if we fail to empathise effectively with those in our care who may not have the long view we embrace.

Stages in our relationship to power

To summarise, here are the stages leading to leadership maturity, and the priorities at each stage:

- *Diplomat:* To belong and maintain the status quo and stability.
- *Expert:* To stand out and gain status.
- *Achiever:* To accomplish goals, gain recognition and rewards.
- *Individualist:* To ensure inclusion, equity and be seen as just.
- *Strategist:* To deliver innovation and transformation.

Note that some crossover exists between these maturity stages and the archetypes from part III – both have a Diplomat, for example, and the Elder archetype is similar to the Strategist stage. The main difference is that the archetypes can appear at any stage in your leadership maturity.

And here's another kicker: we don't ever lose the power motivations as we go through each stage. Our Diplomat need for belonging remains with us, as does the desire for status from the Expert stage. These power goals may be dialled down a little as we mature, but they do not completely leave us. And without vigilance, these motivations leave us vulnerable to Power Games, and the power traps of the shadow archetypes.

Let's look next at how we can build positive aspects of the four spheres to shore up protection against those tempting Power Games.

LOSING SIGHT OF POWER

'I feel so disempowered,' CEO Maja Garcia mumbled. 'I just don't feel like I have much agency right now. I feel so helpless.'

Huw's eyebrows shot up. This was not how he saw her at all. And he knew her better than most. As his business partner and co-founder, they had been through a lot together.

'Maja, I cannot believe I am hearing such poor self-talk coming from you. You've managed an extraordinary feat – as a leader. In just the last six months, you have started a new ground-breaking business, ended a problematic relationship, and built a visionary headquarters for training global world designers.' Huw counted off each achievement on his fingers as he talked. 'You've also been nominated for an industry award and created a movement for new collective, collaborative living on artificial islands. If you had added, "instigated major global reforms for peace keeping", I would not have been surprised.'

Maja looked suitably chastened and smiled weakly.

'You, dear friend, are loaded with agency.'

CHAPTER 4

STOKE YOUR CAULDRON OF COURAGE: BE BRAVE

In the preceding fictional example, we join Maja Garcia and Gaia Enterprises' co-founder, Huw Chan, in the aftermath of a failed community they had built on an artificial island. The experiment had been planned so well, they thought, but ended in tragedy. It's easy to feel powerless when things collapse around us.

To exercise power effectively without losing our moral marbles, we need to master our inner power – our generative power. I like to imagine a giant cauldron over an enormous fire. Inside that cauldron are all of your amazing experiences, accolades, hopes, desires and ambitions. It's all boiling away, fuelled by the creative energy we each possess.

This is the Cauldron of Courage. All you need to do is turn your attention there and feel the comforting heat that rolls from the inside.

Much has been written about this aspect of power, including by me in my first and second books, *Composure* (2015) and *Moments* (2016). And other luminaries also offer a towering body of work, full of gems – hat tip to Brené Brown and Tony Robbins, among others. (The Further Reading list at the end of this book provides a fulsome list of recommendations.)

So rather than regurgitate all the fabulous goodies already out there, in this chapter I run through some summary points and a few additional insights.

Timeless tips

Let's start with some timeless tips for building your Cauldron of Courage.

Timeless Tip 1: Leader, know thyself.

The tip to 'know yourself' as a leader takes you through the gamut of what your values are, your strengths, and your unhelpful habits and patterns. This also includes knowing your stage of leadership maturity, what your current perspective and priorities are, and what your immediate ambitions include. Knowing the ingredients in your Cauldron helps you know what you need to avoid, and what you might need to skim off the surface as the scum boils to the top.

Timeless Tip 2: Leader, prime yourself

If you are to feel powerful and then exercise power (through Conch and Coin), then you need to fire up your Cauldron to the maximum.

This means all the usual strategies of honing your mental acuity through disciplines such as meditation and mindfulness, keeping your body in tiptop shape with exercise, sleep, nutrition, mobility and flexibility, practising emotional regulation with breathing, focus exercises and journalling, and connecting your spiritual self with a higher power and purpose for amplified conviction.

Timeless Tip 3: Leader, nudge yourself

The Cauldron of Courage is about exercising, uh, courage. The folks I work with all want to feel more confident. They say this as if confidence were some elusive grail: 'I would like to feel more confident, and that will solve all my issues'.

Here's the thing, dear leader, confidence is a by-product of courageous action. You need to embrace the suck of doing scary things, whatever that is for you, and work with the consequences of being brave.

We need courage pretty much in all arenas, including courage to take action, courage to speak to a colleague about inappropriate behaviour, courage to throw our hat in the ring for a new role, courage to leave a toxic workplace, courage to try something bold, courage to change a hairstyle, courage to talk with strangers at a networking event. Though the scope and scale of your courage arenas may change, that gut-niggling fear will still be there.

That courage-killer gremlin is there for a reason: to warn us about the impending doom of uncertainty. Sometimes we need to heed its voice, like when we are about to step over the edge of a cliff to our brutalised deaths on the sharp rocks below. And sometimes we just need to talk our gremlin down from an imaginary cliff, like the one that says Harold will swallow us whole if we ask him to share the project guidelines with us.

So work the cliché and build your courage muscle any chance you get.

Additional insights

Here are some additional insights to help you keep your Cauldron bubbling away.

Insight 1: Self-talk for agency, not ego

When it comes to talking about yourself about personal power, do you say to yourself, 'I'm capable'? Or do you say to yourself, 'I am important'?

When we say we're capable, we accentuate our agency.

When we say we're important, we blow our own trumpet.

When you manage power for good and not evil, you want to build up your agency, not your arrogance.

So focus on developing ego for agency and not arrogance.

Insight 2: Self-perception for victor, not victim

Why do we fail to see our own power? We often get stuck on the unpleasantness of now and whatever is currently bothering us. For Maja, she felt stuck, as her pet project had collapsed under the weight of expectations and an experiment gone very badly wrong. She had misjudged the impact of external trends on a fledgling community, Terra Blanca, and underestimated the power of personal interest in sabotaging best-laid plans.

The Terra Blanca Insurrection that was behind the sabotage was indeed a blow to the business and Maja's vision. There was no sugar-coating that. And yet, telling herself she was' disempowered' only reinforced a sense of helplessness for Maja.

Too often, we focus on how far we have to go instead of how far we have come. In doing so, we look externally for validation. At times like these, we should remember the words of philosopher Matshona Dhliwayo:

> *You may not wear a crown, but you're*
> *a king in your own right.*

Insight 3: Use better questions

At times, you may ask why you feel so powerless. A better question and use of language is, 'How can I see myself as powerful?'

For Maja, answering this question could mean digging into the lessons presented. What could she learn from the disaster? What worked well? What could they do differently next time?

Insight 4: Look backwards to leap forwards

Expanding on the previous insight, you can also change your sense of disempowerment by looking further back at all your amazing milestones and achievements. This helps put the setback in a broader context, but this is a morale boost as much as it is perspective-taking. Tallying your wins dials up the release of dopamine and serotonin, giving you a biochemical surge to your Cauldron of Courage.

Insight 5: Redefine success to appreciate effort as well as outcomes

Maja needed to acknowledge all her achievements to date – including the meticulous attention to the design of both the built environment and the governance systems that should, in theory, have worked. Effort has value in itself, even if the outcomes are not what you wanted. While the outcome was tragic, the effort was courageous. Maja would be well-counselled not to throw the baby out with the bathwater as she bemoans her sense of helplessness. They had the courage to try, to dare an ambitious feat of engineering as well as social progress. Success comes from lessons as well as triumphs, and neither comes without effort.

Tending your Cauldron of Courage is a perennial activity, especially if you mean to exercise power with your Coin and Conch.

SIZING UP THE COMPETITION

Jonas Seaborn sized up his competition as he waited for his interview. There was that Italian woman ... what was her name? Gina. She kept to herself, hard as nails. Straight off the streets of Naples. Scrappy.

The other engineer – what happened to him? Jonas wondered. Couldn't take the pressure, no doubt. *He was a scrawny type anyway*, he thought with a twinge of derision.

Jonas rolled his shoulders, his back stiff from his morning punishment in the gym. Jonas knew he was strong and had good presence. Solid. Confident. At least on the outside.

As the son of the famous world designers Don and Jenny Seaborn, he also had fame on his side. The Seaborn name carried a lot of weight in the world design area. Plus, he was an accomplished engineer himself and could fix just about anything on the *Sea Rover*, the Seaborn's floating world, his parents' pride and joy and claim to fame. He hated to admit it, but just this once he was glad to trade on the Seaborn legacy. He really wanted this gig with Gaia. It was building on the Moon! A first. And he'd be the first Seaborn to get there.

CHAPTER 5

ACCUMULATE MORE COIN: BE SEEN

We all seek status. It drives everything from social bonds to workplace performance. The more we have, the better we feel. We revel in the esteem of others not only for the ego satisfaction but also for the privileges and opportunities it brings.

When I think of status, I like to imagine each of us with a medieval leather pouch filled with coins. Before the days of credit cards and paper money, coins were our currency. A hefty Coin bag indicated wealth, and thus power. Those with money, and therefore status, were given more deference and respect. We all want a bulging status Coin bag; it gives us more options.

In this chapter, I run through just how to fill your Coin bag – without letting your quest for status turn toxic.

What fills your Coin bag

So how might you fill up your Coin bag so it's busting at the seams? First, let's take a peek at what might be in that little ole bag.

Packaging

'Packaging' in your Coin bag falls into the category of unearned status, and includes physical attributes such as size, shape, skin colour, gender, sexual orientation and cultural background. Our current social norms and power structures have a hierarchy of status already embedded. If you're white, male, tall, strong, straight and attractive, congratulations – you are at the top of the status tree. In our culture, humans with such vaunted packaging are automatically credited with being more competent and able; therefore, they have a higher status than others, such as their shorter, dark-skinned, plain, female colleagues. This is why the saying goes that women have to work twice as hard just to be seen as equal.

Any degree of differentiation from the status template can be perceived as an impediment. Why? Lordie, it would take a few books to unpack the geo-political, social history of this one.

Is it fair? No.

Can we change this default? Yes.

Is that easy? No. See chapter 14, where I discuss building power structures in teams. It's a long road.

So we start with where we are now: building our status Coin bag.

You may have all the primo, unearned status gold coins. Good for you. Wipe that smug smile off your lips. Focus on how you can help others fill their Coin bag. (See the following chapter for more on developing your Conch.)

Webbing

What holds us together? What allows us to put a front-facing persona into the world? I call these reinforcing structures 'webbing', because they bind many parts of us into a whole. Webbing includes:

- intelligence
- religion or belief system
- spoken/written language skills
- literacy/numeracy
- education.

We can work on all these elements – including our education. Interestingly, not all education is deemed equal. A hierarchy of status is attributed to where you went to school, if you have a university degree and, if so, which university you attended.

Yes, this is snobbish bullshit. But that assessment does not negate its power.

This is the part where I wish I had better news. If you were born with a plastic spoon in your mouth, you will have to work harder at filling your Coin bag.

The only good news is that you can work on it.

Trophies

Here is something else we can work on: achievements. You can work your tail off and, with each accomplishment, hear the clinkety-clink of esteem dropping into your Coin bag. You can hustle and learn and grow and contribute. This is about building your competence and reputation as a great contributor.

Ready to roll your sleeves up and stuff your status Coin bag? Let's do it.

How to fill your status Coin bag – without turning to douchebaggery

You can always turn to dominance, ostracisation, bullying, humiliation and sex to get what you want. If this is you, turn to the shadow archetypes and get thee gone, narcissist psychopath hellion! Your kind ain't wanted around here.

For the moral, upstanding human, what follows is a more dignified pathway. And yes, it can defeat the dark side of the Force.

Self-regulate

Here are some ways to maintain your values and self-regulate as you build your status.

Take stock of your current Coin bag

What have you got in there? What's your packaging like? Consider the following:

- physical attributes (short/tall; big/small; attractiveness)
- gender
- cultural background
- sexual orientation.

Do any of these fall outside of the cultural status norm?

If yes, how can you position your differentiation as an asset?

You're a woman in a male-dominated field? Great! You are a pioneer, you model courage, and you can be the blindspot-revealer for your male colleagues.

You're short? Great! You see what others miss, hear what others don't, and constantly surprise others through being under-estimated. Plus, good things come in small packages.

You're a first-generation immigrant with a different skin colour and accent? Great! You've got stories about different values, different businesses and different systems. You can enrich your current workplace through your lessons and insights.

You have a disability? Great! You model adaptability, resilience and determination that your able-bodied colleagues could only dream of.

This may feel a bit Pollyanna. Discrimination and bias are real – I'm not denying that. But if you're going to battle, *you* need to believe in the amplified power of your difference. Leverage your Cauldron of Courage, and stoke that sucker high.

Maintain strong boundaries

Nothing says 'respect me' more than firm boundaries. Whether they're about time, workload or personal space, clearly defined boundaries communicate self-respect and authority. People are more likely to respect someone who enforces their boundaries consistently. It's a dance, of course. If you make your boundaries too rigid, you will be labelled 'difficult'. If your boundaries are too soft, you will be a pushover. 'Firm' is the Goldilocks 'just right' calibration you need to find.

Stay calm under pressure and control your reactions

I called my first book *Composure: How Centered Leaders Make the Biggest Impact* because enduring presence is the greatest insulation against toxic Power Games. If you are composed and self-assured, you signal strength. Maintaining calm and control during high-stress moments such as criticism or high-stakes negotiations can elevate your status. Avoid overreacting emotionally or becoming defensive. Instead, maintain emotional regulation and respond with measured, thoughtful actions. Others will drop appreciation and respect into your status Coin bag.

Play the competence Power Game

You can also earn status through developing competence and expertise in a skill or hobby – because we all appreciate skilled and competent people. I assumed you're not going for Darth Vader–type domination, and are here on the light side of the Force. Good. So double down on building your expertise and competence to add to your Coin bag.

Learn

Study, take classes, ask for feedback, model other successful people who have the status and competence you aspire to, practise your skills, join discussion groups and ask for extra assignments. Go 'all in' on being the best you can be in your given field.

This is especially important if you have fewer Coins in the packaging and webbing departments. For example, if you do not have English as a first language, how many languages do you speak/read/write? What have these taught you about human dynamics, business relationships and other cultures? How might this be of service to your workplace?

Leverage

Value your time and be selective and thoughtful about who and what you invest it in. Being more discerning with your availability can signal high status, because people perceive busy or selective individuals as more valuable. Be smart about what you take on – one yes often means a million nos, so choose wisely.

To leverage your time even more, use the power of delegation. Delegating tasks effectively can signal status. It shows that you trust others to handle responsibilities and that you are focused on high-level tasks. It also positions you as a leader who can manage resources and people wisely. Be sensible with this – don't offload work to peers because you think you should be delegating. You need to have formal authority to do that, or at least get permission to delegate or share tasks.

Finally, instead of chasing titles or labels, focus on building a portfolio of achievements that showcases your impact. When you are known for tangible results rather than just your position, your status becomes tied to what you've actually accomplished.

Become a resource hub and trend spotter

Share knowledge or advice that adds value to others. Being a go-to source for relevant, insightful information increases your perceived status. Position yourself as the person who knows where to find answers, connections or solutions. Even if you aren't the direct expert, being the person others turn to for guidance on who can help or where to find information builds your status as a trusted resource in your network.

Learn how to spot trends or emerging opportunities before others do. Whether these trends and opportunities are in your industry or within broader social movements, positioning yourself as a forward-thinking individual can enhance your reputation and status.

By building your expertise and knowledge, and acting as resource hub, those status Coins will be clinking away in your growing Coin bag.

Play the character Power Game

It turns out being a kind and compassionate human earns not only respect and Coin, but also bolsters your own sense of well-being. In *Give and Take: Why Helping Others Drives Our Success*, Adam Grant reveals through his research that the most powerful and successful people at work are actually givers: generous folks who give of their time, expertise and resources to help others. They do so with one caveat: not to their own detriment. They take a healthy approach to giving, seek support from others and are happy to ask for help. This is not in a 'tit-for-tat' way, but as a general principle. Much like a pond needs to allow water both in and out to stay healthy, you need to give and receive support and resources to be successful – and build your status.

Be generous with credit

Giving credit to others shows that you are secure in your status, and makes people more inclined to respect and support you. This also enhances your influence. Plus, it boosts others up rather than pushes people down.

Lead with integrity

People respect those who are authentic and trustworthy. Make decisions based on strong ethical principles, and follow through on your promises. Integrity builds long-term status. Stick to your values, do what you say and honour obligations, and you will be far from the traps of skulduggery and cloaked backroom shenanigans.

Be virtuous

We can gain prestige by demonstrating moral fortitude and virtue. When we follow the rules of our community (religious, social, work), we reinforce social agreements or sacred beliefs. This is the Power Game used when we are in the Diplomat stage of leadership maturity (refer to chapter 3). By sticking to the rules, we demonstrate we comply with the norms and support the stability of the group. This can earn us respect and, therefore, status among our peers. Be wary of groupthink and negative peer pressure, however, if you use this tactic.

Play the reputation Power Game

Your reputation can precede you – and help build your status. Use the following to play the reputation Power Game the right way.

Build a strong personal brand

Your brand should reflect your values, strengths and unique expertise, helping you stand out from others in your domain. You may cultivate a reputation for excellence in a specific field, for example. When you load this up with good presence and loads of competence Coin, you become a force to be reckoned with.

Dress the part

Your appearance influences how people perceive your status. Dressing appropriately for your environment – whether in formal or casual settings – can help establish credibility and authority. Superficial? Yes. But what have we seen so far? Just because we don't like something doesn't mean it doesn't exist. First impressions matter, so dress well to boost confidence and appearance, and make the most of your packaging.

Highlight your scarcity

Positioning yourself as someone with limited availability or time increases your perceived value. People are more influenced by those they see as rare or in high demand, so being strategically unavailable can heighten your influence. Don't be a snob here or come across as being 'above it all'. Keep yourself well-occupied with important, high-stakes work that builds competence and earns you accomplishments.

Establish a reputation for generosity

Consistently offer your help, knowledge or resources without expecting immediate returns. Over time, people will associate you with generosity and goodwill, making them more inclined to listen to you and reciprocate by supporting your ideas. Also, this will temper any narrow-eyed judgement of you being too busy to help with organising the morning tea.

Be visible

Consistently share your accomplishments, ideas and contributions. Visibility can be built through speaking engagements, publishing articles, or actively engaging in online and in-person discussions. Talk about your achievements in a humble yet confident way. Let people know what you've accomplished, whether through social media updates, newsletters or conversations.

In *Quietly Powerful*, leadership consultant Megumi Miki challenges the traditional view that leadership requires loudness or extroversion, arguing that quiet leaders can be just as impactful by embracing their authentic selves. She highlights the strengths of quiet leadership, such as deep listening, thoughtfulness, empathy and calmness, which help build trust and create inclusive, collaborative environments. Miki emphasises that quiet leaders focus on impact over visibility, make reflective and deliberate decisions, and lead with authenticity and inner confidence. By valuing these qualities, Miki encourages organisations to challenge the bias favouring extroverted leadership and recognise the power of quiet leaders to create meaningful, lasting change.

For me, this is a situation of yes, *and*.

Yes, quiet achievers have much to offer. Thoughtful, deep listening is powerful when combined with a deep, calm presence.

And we still have systems that favour extroversion and overt confidence. We need to work within the system first before we can change it.

Play the game, and then change the game.

Be wary of letting your competence speak for itself

In our current systems, too many humble, virtuous leaders are being left behind while their more brazen, less competent colleagues snap up the opportunities.

Being good at your job does not mean you will get promoted. You need to speak up. You need to advocate for yourself. You need to turn this passive power of status, your now-hefty Coin bag, into active power.

In short, you need to blow your Conch – and I get to that in the next chapter.

Before we move on, however, we need to be mindful of other folks playing different kinds of status Power Games: toxic ones.

Toxic status Power Games

Status as a force is underrated, and most people deny they give it much consideration. When I first started researching and talking about status, I learned threats to status were often unconsciously seen as threats to our very survival. The work of neuroscientist David Rock identified status as one of the first triggers of fight, flight or freeze reactions – otherwise known as an amygdala hijack.

But when I've asked groups 'who feels riled by threats to status?', people rarely, save the honest few, raise their hand. It seems gauche to do so. After all, if I care about status, I might be seen as a self-absorbed selfish prig.

And yet the research shows that status is an integral part of our journey as a species. We have been collaborative ever since we crawled into caves. As we came together to survive, we also competed for approval and acclaim from our fellow group members. Greater approval gave us greater access to resources, a better selection of potential mates, and better opportunities for our offspring. Status had, and still does have, currency. Back then, reduced status could result in a very real threat to survival – being excluded from the group and left to fend for ourselves. From a leadership maturity point of view, loss of status represents a blow to our sense of self as status is a primary driver at this stage. Being excluded as a result of loss of status is detrimental to the Diplomat stage (the precursor to Expert stage) and our sense of security. So, losing status threatens not only our identity but our safety. Egad!

More than approval and access to resources, though, the pursuit of status gives us emotional satisfaction, because it supports our need for meaning and purpose. Our pursuits bring accomplishments, acclaim and esteem. Status may be a proxy to the work itself, but it still drives at least a portion of our effort. In other words, status is integral to our sense of self-worth.

So why does status get a bad rap? Because people play toxic Power Games with status. Let's look at some of the most damaging.

Pushing people down to boost ourselves up

Instead of earning status through good deeds, accomplishments and contribution to the group, some prigs default to dominance to conflate their rank. They apply a 'If you're down, I'm up' type of equation.

Dominance may include physical violence as well as ostracisation, bullying and humiliation. This kind of game works temporarily, as people tend to comply with coercive bullies, reinforcing the bully's sense and demonstration of power. But it's a short-lived and, ultimately, unsuccessful strategy. Why? Because going around beating up and threatening people all the time is incredibly energy-intensive. Not to mention the resentment it cultivates in others.

Loss of status creates a**holes

The fear of losing status may promote unsociable and negative behaviours. Journalist Will Storr's research shows that this can differ between men and women. Men may default to dominance or violence to defend their status while women might use social tools such as gossip and undermining and other social exclusion tactics to suppress rivals. Nasty, either way.

Chasing status creates creeps

Social media can accelerate toxic status Power Games. An increase in the number of our followers, likes and comments can feel like an increase in our prestige. We can also amplify our achievements on social media or use virtue signalling.

The good ole humble brag positions our moral fortitude alongside a favourite charity we support. Many a CEO has been accused of 'virtue signalling' in undertaking events like the CEO Sleepout, for example. Much like greenwashing, where a business's support for environmental causes is superficial, virtue signalling may reveal only a cursory and self-oriented interest in the cause. While many CEOs are genuinely philanthropic and altruistic, others are riding the status wave by hyping these initiatives.

Toxic status Power Games on social media can also devolve to cyber bullying, gaslighting and reputation assault. It's a festy cesspool for keyboard warriors.

Unearned blind status

As discussed earlier in this chapter, unearned social status comes from aspects such as race, gender, cultural background, physical attributes and privilege. Societal cultural expectations dictate the status of each of these aspects, and are particular to individual communities. If we fit into the cultural norm of what is perceived as pleasant, attractive or esteemed, then we may be granted status surreptitiously. This is what we refer to now as 'privilege'.

This unearned status creates empathy blind spots, because sometimes we are not aware of how much easier things are for us if we fit into the cultural norm of 'high status'. We don't get questioned extensively in airport queues, we don't get pulled over more often by police, others don't hurry away from us as we walk down the street, people don't catcall or hurl abuse at us as we go about our daily lives. Instead, we walk through public spaces unhurried and hassle free, we are welcomed in venues and service personnel greet us warmly.

This is a particularly insidious toxic status Power Game because those with privilege are often blind to the entire game, participating in it with unconscious bias, enjoying the benefits of having great packaging, webbing, and easily gained trophies.

Unfair use of status

Positional authority and status can lead to the exploitation of others. This may be subtle, such as expecting others to clean up our coffee cups after a meeting, or more sinister, such as using our status as the boss/teacher/expert to lure or pressure others into inappropriate sexual relationships. Many workplaces ban fraternisation and relationships between management and interns/junior staff for a reason: a power imbalance exists that can lead to other unethical flexing, such as favouring the more junior lover, securing them opportunities ahead of others. It goes both ways: the person with status may use their position to coerce a sexual relationship, while those with lower status may use sex to secure privileges and opportunities.

Ugh.

Of course, good systems can help inoculate against these kinds of toxic Power Games. In the meantime, we can use the solid Coin we have built for ourselves and lean into active power – using our Conch to wield power well.

Let's take a look.

WHAT ABOUT *ME*?

Claire Edwards fumed. She closed the door to her private accommodation, sat at her desk, and stared out the window that overlooked the central green plaza of the Gaia training centre. The centre she had helped design.

Maja was not taking her opinion seriously. As the chief operating officer, she had a right to express her opinion. And Maja was usually more open to suggestions. But this time she was almost dismissive of Claire's concerns.

Where was she going wrong? Was Maja just in a bad mood? Or had she become blinkered by her obsession with this project?

Claire rubbed her forehead, easing the tension that clung to her like a leech.

Going to the Moon. It was a folly. And well beyond Gaia's founding purpose of protecting the Earth.

Maybe if she waited it out, tried again, Maja would come around and see reason. After all, Claire had worked diligently to build the Gaia training school right alongside Maja. Sooner or later, Maja was bound to name her the successor to her role as CEO. Surely her experience and track record would speak for itself. She was the obvious candidate. Maja would surely see that.

Claire just had to keep doing her job, and doing it well, like she always did. Cream rises to the top, so they say.

CHAPTER 6

DEVELOP YOUR CONCH: BE HEARD

After all the hard work you've done building your Coin bag, the biggest mistake you can make is sitting around waiting to be noticed. The passive social power aspect of developing status works up to a point. After that, something more is needed – and too many leaders have been bypassed for not being more vocal as well as visible.

Hence, time to develop your Conch.

The Conch has long symbolised power, voice and authority across cultures. In Hinduism and Buddhism, it represents spiritual awakening and the spread of truth, while in Mesoamerican cultures (such as the Mayan and Aztec), it was used in religious ceremonies and as a call to action. Historically, conch shells served as communication tools, signalling gatherings or important events. In modern literature, such as William Golding's *Lord of the Flies*, the conch symbolises democracy and the right to speak. Today, it remains a metaphor for influence and inclusive leadership, reflecting the importance of giving others a voice in decision-making processes, and claiming our voice at the table.

We also need to make the distinction between using the Conch and 'blowing one's own trumpet'. The Conch is about authority and inclusion in group dynamics, while the latter focuses on self-promotion and personal recognition. The Conch symbolises a more balanced, respectful use of voice, whereas trumpet-blowing can imply a more assertive or self-centred use of influence.

Getting heard the right way

We know the narcissist will be blowing trumpets while decent heart-centred leaders like you will be developing and using their Conch.

So, how do you get heard?

Master your message

Those who wield the Conch will have something meaningful to say, and will say it well. Let's start with the meaningful part first.

Create a shared mission

Frame your influence attempts in terms of collective goals. People are more willing to act when they feel like they are part of something bigger. Use inclusive language like 'we' and 'together' to build a sense of shared purpose.

Tell stories that resonate

People are more easily influenced when they see that you share their values. Tell stories that resonate with the principles or ideals your audience holds dear. When they see alignment in values, they are more likely to follow your lead.

Telling compelling stories not only engages others, but also makes you more memorable. Those who can tell great stories often command attention and respect, which builds their status in social and professional circles – and their ability to use the Conch.

Use metaphors and analogies

Metaphors and analogies make complex ideas relatable and easier to grasp. When you can simplify difficult concepts into something familiar, people are more likely to be persuaded by your message.

Ask thought-provoking questions

Instead of only offering answers or insights, ask deep, reflective questions that encourage others to think more critically. This positions you as someone who values intellect and stimulates thoughtful discussions, elevating your status as a thinker.

Use the power of 'because'

According to research, people are more likely to be influenced when you give them a reason – even if it's a simple one. Phrasing requests with 'because' (for example, 'Could you do this because …') can increase compliance by providing a rationale, even if it's obvious.

Use silence

High-status individuals don't always feel the need to fill silences with talk. Practising the art of silence in conversations can make you appear more thoughtful and in control. Pausing before responding shows that you value your words and can make others pay more attention when you speak.

Silence can even be more powerful than words in certain situations. Pausing before responding creates a space that others feel the need to fill, often revealing more or becoming more receptive to your influence.

Adapt your communication style

Tailor your language and approach to fit the communication style of the person you want to influence. Some people respond better to facts and logic, while others are more moved by emotion and personal stories.

Prime for persuasion

Psychologist Robert Cialdini is well known as the master of influence. His seminal work is *Influence: The Psychology of Persuasion*, which I mention later in this chapter. But let's look first at what Cialdini highlights as possible before the persuasion even starts. In *Pre-Suasion: A Revolutionary Way to Influence and Persuade*, Cialdini explores how to set the stage for successful influence before the persuasive message is even delivered. He focuses on the concept that what happens before the persuasion attempt can dramatically influence the outcome. This is called 'priming'.

Here are the key points:

- *Attention is key:* Cialdini emphasises that what you focus someone's attention on right before persuasion can steer their thoughts and emotions. By guiding someone's attention to the right elements (such as success, safety or scarcity), you can shape how they respond to a subsequent message.

- *The power of associations:* You can enhance your persuasive efforts by associating your message with positive concepts or emotions. For instance, connecting a brand or idea with feelings of warmth, safety or achievement can make the audience more favourable towards the message.

- *Unity as a principle:* In addition to the six principles of persuasion outlined by Cialdini in *Influence*, in *Pre-Suasion* he introduces a new principle – unity. This refers to the idea that people are more likely to be influenced by others they consider part of their group or tribe. First creating a sense of belonging or shared identity boosts receptiveness to the message.

- *Framing the message:* The way information is framed matters greatly. For example, framing a message in terms of what can be lost (and so tuning into most people's loss aversion bias) often works better than framing it in terms of potential gains.

- *Timing and context:* The timing and context in which a message is delivered are crucial. By controlling the environment or the sequence of events leading up to the persuasion attempt, you can influence the mindset of your audience to be more open to the message.

- *Moment of persuadability:* At certain moments people are more susceptible to influence. Cialdini argues in *Pre-Suasion* that identifying and leveraging these moments – such as when people are already thinking about an idea related to your message – can greatly enhance the effectiveness of your persuasion efforts.

- *Use of language and cues:* Specific words, phrases or even images can prime people towards a desired thought process. Subtle linguistic or visual cues can lead people to think in ways that align with the intended persuasion, such as using words that evoke safety, risk or urgency.

In *Pre-Suasion*, Cialdini takes persuasion beyond just the message itself, highlighting the importance of what happens before the message is delivered. He emphasises the role of context, timing and the careful orchestration of attention in making people more likely to say 'yes'.

Nurture relationships and networks

It's not just what you know and how you say it that affects your influence; it's who you know as well. You can wield your Conch better if you have more people who know, like and trust you. Let's move on to what Cialdini has to say about this topic.

Build relationship capital

You can build relationships – and so a more powerful Conch – through the following:

- *Reciprocity:* People feel a strong need to repay favours or kindnesses, even if unsolicited. When someone gives us something, we are hardwired to feel obliged to give something back, which can be leveraged in marketing, sales and negotiation. You can build up your reciprocity bank by giving colleagues gifts, recommendations and suggestions, or even lending them a pen, book or other items.

- *Commitment and consistency:* Once people make a choice or take a stand, they are motivated to act consistently with that commitment. Getting someone to agree to a small initial request increases the likelihood they'll comply with larger requests in the future. When we ask someone to do a favour for us, they may at first hesitate due to being unsure of the obligation; however, they will still be drawn into the ask because all of us like to feel important. When someone asks a favour, we feel honoured and we get a little surge of pride. Asking for a small favour – such as, 'Can you watch my bag while I duck to the loo?' – is pretty innocuous. It can, however, lead to bigger and bigger asks being granted, until you might ask to be introduced to the CEO or another power broker.

- *Liking:* We are more easily persuaded by people we like. Cialdini argues that we are more likely to say 'yes' to people we find physically attractive or similar to us, along with people who compliment us, or show cooperation and goodwill. Though attractiveness is subjective, we can emphasise our assets by being well groomed and well dressed as a starting point – and research shows that people want these attributes from their leaders. Regardless, we can win esteem and build our Conch by being gracious, giving compliments and showing goodwill towards others.

Network strategically

It's all about who you know. Some people call them 'sponsors'; you might call them mentors or advocates. Whatever you call them, having friends in high places is advantageous. These people can open doors and make important introductions.

Here's how to be strategic in your networking:

- *Be selective:* Build relationships with influential people in your industry or community. Being associated with high-status individuals can elevate your own status by association. Be intentional about who you associate with and how you present your social network. Seek relationships with respected or influential individuals, while distancing yourself from negative associations.

- *Act as a connector:* High-status individuals often act as bridges between others. Introduce people in your network who could benefit from knowing each other. When you help others succeed, your status rises within your community. Be the connector in your network, remembering that influence doesn't always come from what you know but from whom you can connect. By facilitating valuable introductions and helping others network, you gain influence as someone who holds the key to important relationships.

Be a good human

Here are some more tips for building influence and strengthening the wind in your Conch:

- *Create small wins for others:* Help people achieve small, meaningful successes. When others feel you've contributed to their victories, even in minor ways, they're more likely to listen to and be influenced by you in the future.

- *Be curious about others:* Ask questions that spark curiosity or challenge existing assumptions. This not only shows that you're thinking deeply, but also positions you as someone who can broaden others' perspectives. People are naturally drawn to those who provoke curiosity.

- *Embrace vulnerability:* Showing vulnerability strategically can build influence. Admitting mistakes or showing you don't have all the answers can make you more relatable, which means others are more likely to trust you and follow your lead. This works best if you have already demonstrated competence. Unproven leaders who go around saying they don't know and that they've stuffed up do not earn respect or trust.

Develop charisma through warmth and competence

One of my favourite books on practical influence is Vanessa Van Edwards' *Cues: Master the Secret Language of Charismatic Communication*. She highlights how mastering both verbal and non-verbal cues can enhance your charisma, likability and authority.

Central to her work is the research she did on charisma, which highlighted that charisma is not just for the singing and dancing, show-pony, gregarious extroverts. Charisma is about how we show up – and, specifically, how we signal *warmth* and *competence*. She calls these signals 'cues'.

Here's how your warmth and competence combine to create charisma:

- *Warmth cues:* These are signals of friendliness, empathy and trustworthiness. Warmth cues include smiling, nodding, open body language and maintaining eye contact. People are more likely to trust and feel connected to individuals who exhibit warmth.

- *Competence cues:* These signals convey confidence, skill and authority. Competence cues include standing tall, using deliberate gestures, having a strong vocal tone, and using clear, assertive language. These cues help others perceive you as capable and knowledgeable.

- *Balancing warmth and competence:* The key to charisma is striking the right balance between warmth and competence. Too much warmth without competence can make you seem friendly but not authoritative, while too much competence without warmth can make you seem intimidating or unapproachable.

Cues are powerful signals. Both verbal and non-verbal cues send signals about your intentions, emotions and confidence. Learning to master these signals allows you to control how you are perceived by others. Let's look at the different types of cues.

Non-verbal cues

Outside of what you say, people are also picking up your non-verbal cues, as follows:

- *Body language:* The way you position yourself communicates volumes. Open, relaxed body language indicates confidence and comfort, while closed-off gestures (such as crossed arms or slouching) can signal defensiveness or insecurity. Yes, the research actually does show that crossed arms can be off-putting.

- *Facial expressions:* Facial expressions are crucial for conveying emotions. Smiling is a universal cue for warmth and friendliness, while frowning or avoiding eye contact can make you seem distant or uninterested. My favourite tip is the 'flexed eyelid'. To do this, squint at something over in the corner of the room. This is the flexed eyelid (otherwise known as the 'Blue Steel' look). Using this signals competence through indicating you are really narrowing your focus to concentrate.

- *Eye contact:* Maintaining the right amount of eye contact can convey both warmth and confidence. Too little eye contact may make you seem untrustworthy or uninterested, while too much can feel uncomfortable or overly intense. Obviously, this is cultural-context dependent. Many cultures deem eye contact as rude or salacious. Do your research before your keen eye contact results in an offence you hadn't anticipated.

Vocal cues

How you talk also creates certain cues, through the following:

- *Tone of voice:* A strong, controlled voice conveys authority and competence, while a softer, warmer tone can evoke trust and empathy. It's important to vary your tone based on the context and the message you're delivering.

- *Pace and volume:* Speaking too quickly can come across as nervous, while speaking too slowly may seem disengaging. Speaking at a moderate pace and volume reflects confidence and helps keep people engaged.

- *Pitch:* Lower pitch can convey authority, while higher pitch can sometimes suggest excitement or friendliness. Being aware of the pitch of your voice and modulating it can help you appear both warm and competent. And for goodness' sake, make sure you finish your sentences with a downward tone instead of an up-flection like you're asking a question.

Verbal cues

Of course, *what* you say still matters, so keep in mind the following:

- *Choice of words:* Using strong, confident language can boost the perception of your competence. Avoiding filler words (such as 'um' or 'like') and using precise language increases your credibility.

- *Compliments and empathy:* Verbal cues that convey warmth include giving genuine compliments, showing empathy and asking thoughtful questions. This helps build rapport and trust with others.

- *Storytelling:* Telling compelling stories can engage an audience, make you more relatable, and demonstrate both warmth and competence by showcasing your expertise while connecting emotionally.

Written verbal cues

You can use charisma in your writing too by using a balance of competence and warmth signals. Your email correspondence can open with a friendly Hello and close with a Regards. You may inquire after someone's health or say something like, 'I trust this finds you well'. These are warmth signals. You don't want to go overboard, especially with someone you're trying to build rapport with, and who has a higher status or authority. You then add competence signals by sticking to the point, being succinct and being direct without being rude.

When it comes to writing anything, be brief. 'Nuff said.

Respond to situational cues

When sending out cues, you need to be conscious of your social setting and the cues you're getting back, as follows:

- *Context matters:* The effectiveness of cues depends on the context. For example, warmth cues may be more effective in personal relationships, while competence cues are essential in leadership or high-stakes professional settings.

- *Reading others' cues:* Success in communication also involves recognising and responding to other people's cues. This means paying attention to their body language, tone and expressions, and then adapting your approach accordingly.

Toxic Power Games using the Conch

Did you feel a little icky reading anything in this chapter? Perhaps you found the suggestions were bordering on being disingenuous or … manipulative! Just like toadies can use status in an underhanded way, influence can easily turn to manipulation when using the Conch.

This is an important time to remember the difference between *influence* and *manipulation*. Influence is helping someone to do or think something that is good for them as well as good for you. Manipulation is about getting others to do something that is not always good for them, but is good for you. Beware of the temptation to turn to manipulation if you are not making any headway with a full Coin bag and diligent use of Conch. (Turn to part III and the chapters on archetypes and their shadows for your official heads-up.)

In the meantime, remember that successful influence using your Conch does not mean dominating the conversation. Nowhere in this chapter did I say, 'Stand up and talk over people, and be loud and aggressive'. True influence doesn't require volume; it's about timing, presence and finesse. A fine line exists between patiently waiting your turn to speak and seizing the moment. Think of dancing on this line as a verbal ballet, where you gracefully create space for others while confidently claiming your own. You can lean in slightly, signalling readiness. You can take a breath as if you're about to speak or raise a finger or hand, signalling that you've got something important to contribute. These non-verbal cues, as much as verbal ones, make your presence felt before you even utter a word.

If you find yourself unable to get a word in because someone else is dominating the conversation, try these conversation interrupters to respectfully claim some air time:

- *Lean in, raise a finger, and then speak:* Try interrupting with, 'If I may, I have a suggestion that might be of service.'
- *Use open body language:* Lean slightly forward, make eye contact and smile to signal that you're ready to speak.
- *Use pacing:* If the conversation has no pauses, strategically create one. Start speaking softly just after the dominant speaker takes a breath. Timing your entry during a natural pause shows control and patience.
- *Use empathy as a bridge:* Say, 'I hear you, and here's something that builds on that idea', instead of using dismissive phrases like, 'I hear you, *but*', which can feel confrontational.
- *Validate before contributing:* 'I appreciate the direction you're going in, *and* I'd like to add an alternative perspective that could enrich the discussion.'
- *Use subtle interjections:* For instance, 'I'd love to build on that point', or 'That resonates with me. May I add something?'

Avoiding phrases like, 'With all due respect' is essential, because these often signal a dismissal of the other person's point. Instead, think about framing your contribution as collaborative rather than combative. For instance, as outlined in the preceding points, using the word 'and' instead of 'but' invites dialogue and signals a willingness to engage productively.

By mastering these conversational techniques, you can assert yourself without dominating or overpowering others, making space for both influence and inclusivity. Influence doesn't always come from speaking the loudest but from speaking with purpose, presence and clarity.

By building Coins and exercising your Conch, you may end up with that hallowed Crown.

And then the game changes. Let's take a look.

EMPIRE WITHOUT BORDERS

Aryanna Sharif shook the hands of the other Lunar Commissioners one by one, her long slender fingers firm in their grasp, elegant and strong. She remained resolute and implacable in their congratulations. They had nominated her Chair of the Lunar Commission and, at last, her plans were coming together.

Aryanna Industries had significant investments in the space sector, including the recent decision to back Gaia Enterprises' bid to win the Olympus Project and build the first community on the Moon. Now, as Chair, the path was clear to see her terraforming and community building ambitions come to fruition. A frisson of excitement danced along her spine. The worlds were at her feet.

CHAPTER 7

USE THE POWER OF THE CROWN WISELY: BEWARE

Congratulations! You've been granted authority. Maybe you've got a new promotion, you've been made a manager, or even a CEO or Chair.

You now have *power over* others. You can make decisions on careers, resources, directions and opportunities. Your pay packet is larger, and you get invited into meetings you haven't been to before. You might have a new office, and perhaps access to free parking and a company credit card. People look at you differently. A certain amount of deference, a sheepish guarded surrender now occurs in your presence. People take you more seriously. They ask your opinion more. You are told about certain behind-the-scenes issues and you secretly zing with smug satisfaction about this whole new world of privilege and access. Your chest puffs just a little, you walk a little taller and strut a little more. You feel like a somebody. You feel proud. You've worked hard for this. You deserve this …

Alright now, back to Earth. Get off the dopamine-frenzied power racehorse and jump back on the workhorse. Your brain and body have just been jazzed up on power and the danger is high that you'll become a tyrant. The stepping stone to that? A strong sense of entitlement. As William Shakespeare reminds us in *Henry IV, Part 2*, 'Uneasy lies the head that wears a crown'.

The Crown and entitlement

I know you think this sense of entitlement (and tyrant temptation) won't happen to you. Maybe it won't. But to be sure, let's itemise the warning signs:

- *Detachment from reality:* Up in your leadership ivory tower, you may forget what it's like at the coal face. You may become detached from the struggles of your team and start to feel the 'us and them' divide swamp around you like a moat.

- *Sense of immunity:* Now that you're a 'leader', you may feel your role offers you some sort of protection. The organisation protects their own, right? Especially those in elevated roles. This may drive you to make unscrupulous decisions at worst, and morally flexible ones at best.

- *Personalisation of success:* You may take credit for your team's accomplishments, basking in the glory of their collective contributions. After all, it was your leadership that got them as far as they did.

- *Excessive control:* Maybe you're a more nervous leader, wary of delegation lest your people stuff up. You worry about your team delivering the expected results so you micromanage them and stifle innovation so nothing rocks the boat. Or, worse yet, maybe an up-and-coming high performer is threatening to upstage you, so you undermine them, sideline them or squash their ambition.

For even more sobering observations, refer to chapter 1, where I run through the negative effects of power.

How to avoid being a tyrant

Let's be sure to take the antidote potions to the temptations of the tyrant. Here they are.

Take a big bite of humble pie

As I wrote about in *People Stuff*, the Elder archetype is central to making wise and compassionate decisions. Its shadow archetype is the Tyrant, and to avoid slipping into this shadow archetype, we need to be mindful of hubris, that combination of arrogance and pride that blows our ego up like a balloon. Humility is knowing that you can't do everything, you can't do it alone, and your role is to serve and make things easier for others.

Leadership is a privilege, not for privileges. With leadership comes great responsibility. So, be humble. Acknowledge your team members' contributions, distribute credit fairly and keep asking, 'How can I help make your job better and easier?'

I love this quote from Frederick the Great, King of Prussia from 1740 to 1786: 'A crown is merely a hat that lets the rain in'.

Earning the title through his military achievements and successful rule, 'Frederick the Great' transformed Prussia into a major European power and left a lasting impact on its culture and society. While admired for his intellect and accomplishments, he was also criticised for his authoritarian rule and involvement in wars that caused a significant loss of life. He was aware enough to be mindful of delusions of grandeur and the responsibility that comes with authority.

Be a power cog, not a power hog

The difference between being a power cog and power hog is the difference between collaborative and self-centred leadership. As a power hog, you hoard authority for personal gain, stifling others. As a power cog, on the other hand, you see yourself as part of a larger system, using your position to empower the team and foster shared responsibility. By contributing to collective success and distributing leadership, power cogs create sustainable, high-functioning organisations where everyone can thrive. True leadership comes from enabling others, not monopolising power.

Be a power maker, not a power monger

Are you creating power or hoarding it? As a power maker, you grow power in others by fostering collaboration, sharing knowledge and enabling team members to lead, creating long-term, sustainable leadership. In contrast, as a power monger, you hoard power, manipulate situations to maintain control and focus on personal dominance, often stifling creativity and eroding trust. While power makers build resilient organisations through generosity and shared responsibility, power mongers create competitive, fear-driven environments that ultimately limit growth and innovation.

Help people play with power

One of your first duties as a leader is to grow more leaders. If you want to change the narrative in your workplace, and its relationship with power more broadly, you need to help people 'play with power' and avoid destructive power plays. You can do this by creating environments where power is understood, shared and used constructively rather than competitively. Here are some ways to do so.

- *Clarify power dynamics:* Make power structures visible and discuss them openly. Help people understand where power comes from in the organisation (for example, formal roles, expertise and influence) and how it can be used positively. By demystifying power, you reduce the potential for covert power plays.

- *Talk about power:* Promote open conversations about how power is distributed and used. When people understand that power is not a limited resource, more collaborative relationships can emerge rather than secretive power struggles.

- *Help others play with power:* Encourage people to take on leadership roles, even in informal or project-based settings. Give them the chance to 'play with power' in a safe environment where they can make decisions, influence outcomes and see the effects of their authority without fear of failure. Embed fierce and frank feedback as part of the entire team's process for growth and learning. By debriefing the leadership experience with everyone, all learn.

- *Emphasise collaboration over competition:* Emphasise that power can grow through collaboration with collective influence and impact. Encourage shared decision-making, where power is distributed across the team. Reward and recognise collective success, as well as individual contributions.

- *Use persuasion power, not just positional power:* Help people to balance formal authority (the 'Crown') with informal influence (the 'Conch'). When people learn to combine both forms of power, they become adept at navigating different situations without relying solely on title or status. Help others to learn how to make decisions and then communicate this well with engaging stories that bring the decisions to life.

Balance the Crown and the Conch

Sometimes you need to use your Crown. We rely on authority when urgent decisions are required, like during a crisis. Additionally, when ambiguity threatens to swallow the team, we can use authority to set clear direction, and clarify roles, responsibilities and expectations. You might also need to use the Crown to enforce policies and standards, and uphold rules or organisational principles that might not be popular but are critical for fairness or compliance (for example, safety regulations or legal requirements).

As a leader with formal authority, you can also use your Conch. You can rely on influence to build consensus and engagement. Here, influence is more effective than authority. People are more motivated and committed when they feel like they've been part of the process. If you are trying to foster innovation and creativity, this is best done with influence and encouraging all to participate than to dictate a particular outcome. Conch is most useful during major change, when you can dial up your empathy, listening skills and compassionate communication.

Effective leaders often start with influence – persuading, aligning and motivating their teams – and reserve authority for moments when it's crucial to ensure adherence to decisions or to resolve disputes quickly.

Power traps and escape moves for the Elder to avoid becoming the Tyrant

These strategies help the Elder remain connected to compassion and wisdom, pulling them back from the Tyrant trap of power and hubris.

Power trap #1: Monopolise decision-making

Beware of when you start to hoard decision-making, dismissing others' input based on your sense of superiority.

Here are your escape moves from this trap:

- *Practise self-reflection:* Regularly ask yourself, 'Am I listening to others? Am I valuing their input as much as my own?' Schedule check-ins with trusted peers to gain feedback about your behaviour.

- *Encourage open dialogue:* Create space for others to contribute their perspectives. Remind yourself that diversity of thought strengthens decision-making.

- *Acknowledge limitations:* Be open about the areas where you need advice or assistance, signalling that you don't have all the answers and value the expertise of your team.

Power trap #2: All about the numbers

In this trap, you can start to rely too much on data and logic, ignoring emotional or ethical considerations in decision-making.

Here are the escape moves:

- *Engage in empathy-building exercises:* Spend time understanding how decisions impact people on a human level. Ask yourself, 'Who will be affected by this, and how?'

- *Consult ethical guidelines:* Before making major decisions, review the ethical implications. Invite perspectives from people focused on organisational culture and employee wellbeing to balance data with compassion.

- *Use storytelling:* Bring narratives of the people or teams affected into decision-making processes, ensuring that empathy plays a central role in your choices.

Power trap #3: I know best

We may start to isolate ourselves when falling into this trap, acting as the sole source of wisdom and refusing to consult others.

Escape moves are as follows:

- *Create advisory groups:* Formalise input from a group of trusted peers or colleagues who can offer diverse perspectives on critical issues. Set up regular meetings to consult them before making decisions.

- *Welcome constructive challenge:* Invite and genuinely consider dissenting opinions, recognising that critique sharpens wisdom. Consider feedback as a tool for growth, not a threat to authority.

- *Rotate decision-making responsibilities:* Involve others in making final calls on significant projects or initiatives, allowing them to contribute their wisdom and expertise.

Power trap #4: Centralised control

As you consolidate power, you can start to centralise decision-making and stifle innovation to preserve control.

Here are your escape moves:

- *Delegate effectively:* Gradually shift decision-making power to your team. Start with smaller projects to build trust and encourage autonomy. Reassure yourself that empowering others doesn't diminish your authority. It strengthens the organisation.

- *Establish shared leadership:* Create systems where decisions are made collaboratively, reducing the pressure to be the sole leader and allowing others to step up.

- *Recognise and reward innovation:* Shift your focus from preserving control to fostering creativity. Encourage your team to explore new ideas and reward calculated risks, even if they deviate from your vision.

Power trap #5: Legacy obsession

In this trap, you can become fixated on building your personal legacy, imposing your vision at the expense of others' contributions.

Escape moves are as follows:

- *Emphasise collective legacy:* Remind yourself that the true legacy of leadership is empowering others to carry on the mission. Share credit widely and focus on developing future leaders.

- *Mentor future generations:* Shift your energy towards mentoring others, ensuring that your values and wisdom are passed on through them, rather than enforcing a rigid vision.

- *Celebrate diverse contributions:* Regularly highlight the impact of different team members and celebrate their achievements, moving the spotlight away from yourself.

Power trap #6: Hero complex

In this trap, you can start to buy in to your own bullshit. A bristle of pride in accomplishments becomes a sense of entitlement and hubris. The organisation really is amazing due to your efforts. You have held it all together. You have fronted up, taken on the risks, weathered the storms, and are still standing. You deserve to be appreciated and honoured. They couldn't have done it without you …

You get the picture. You've got to pop that hot-air balloon before it carries you up, up and away into puffery.

Here are your escape moves:

- *Cultivate humility and gratitude:* Reflect on your impact, remembering that leadership is about the collective, not just personal success. Practising gratitude for the contributions of others keeps your focus on the team and helps deflate an inflated ego.

- *Engage in humility practices:* Adopt practices such as openly admitting mistakes or seeking feedback from the team. This regular reminder of human fallibility helps keep us grounded.

- *Shift the focus from 'I' to 'we':* Consciously credit the team for successes and view your own role as a facilitator rather than as the central figure. Reflecting on how others have contributed to success keeps the ego balanced.

- *Mentor others as a legacy:* Instead of seeking personal recognition, focus on mentoring future leaders as part of your legacy. This reframing of legacy from individual success to collective development will reduce the focus on personal accolades.

Power trap #7: Rusted on

You've been doing the job so long, you can't imagine anything else. You may not want to do anything else. Your ideas have been great, and you've led the organisation from strength to strength – or at least out of some dark places. But what if you can't do it again? What if this is the best you've got? What if you don't have any other ideas? Better to stay where you are and ride out the time to retirement. You've earned the right to rest on your laurels ... right?

Complacency is poisonous.

Here are your moves to escape this trap:

- *Reflect on the bigger picture:* Revisit your original motivations and values. Why did you step into leadership? What impact did you hope to make? Reflecting on these questions can reignite a sense of purpose.

- *Seek out optimistic peers:* Deliberately engage with colleagues or mentors who are energised by the work and who bring fresh, positive perspectives. This can help spark new ideas and energy.

- *Focus on the future:* In moments of cynicism, consciously shift focus from past disappointments to future possibilities. Ask, 'What could be different in the next phase?' This forward-thinking mindset breaks the cycle of dwelling on negative experiences.

- *Pursue personal growth:* Engage in learning opportunities – whether through new books, courses or experiences – that rekindle the joy of discovery. Investing in growth and curiosity can reignite passion for leadership.

- *Take a break:* If possible, step back briefly from the day-to-day pressures of leadership. A sabbatical, short break, or even a change in routine can provide much-needed space for reflection and rejuvenation, helping to dispel feelings of burnout and negativity.

Remember – attaining authority is energising and rewarding. It is also riddled with the perils of power. With diligence and care, you may yet avoid becoming the tyrant you never wanted to be. Here's another reminder from a past monarch – this time, Queen Elizabeth I, from 1601:

> *To be a king and wear a crown is a thing more*
> *glorious to them that see it than it is pleasant*
> *to them that bear it.*

Well done! You've mastered the art of stoking your Cauldron of Courage, you've filled your status Coin bag to the brim, you've blown your Conch, and now your head is uneasy with the privilege and responsibility of wearing the Crown.

But what about all the other folks who are more Machiavelli than Mahatma Gandhi? How do you contend with *their* Power Games?

Roll your sleeves up; we're digging into the tough stuff.

PART III

POWER GAMES IN ARCHETYPES

Power Games emerge when a team or organisation's systems are not properly organised to prevent the slip into the 'shadow' side – the dark or selfish side of human nature. In part IV, I delve into how to revamp those systems; however, before we get to that point, it's important to note how you might deploy counter moves to any shadowy, shitty behaviour you experience in the workplace. Unfortunately, these experiences are all too common, so you need to have some resilience and dexterity in disarming this arsehole behaviour right away, even if you don't yet have the clout or Crown to change the systems.

Survival first, revolution later.

In my experience and research, I have found that many jerks start out well intentioned. They embody a healthy archetype, and then may fall into a shadow version of that archetype, using nasty Power Games to get what they want. I first explored five key archetypes in *People Stuff*, and touched on their shadow. These archetypes, and their shadows, are as follows:

- Elder/Tyrant
- Warrior/Bully
- Diplomat/Manipulator
- Guardian/Fanatic
- Pioneer/Gambler.

In the chapters in this part, I unpack the Power Games that tend to emerge with the shadow side of each archetype, and the counter moves you can use – especially if you do not have a Crown and cannot use authority to stamp out the appalling behaviour.

Office politics begone! Here we go.

BILLIONAIRE TECH BROS BOUND BEYOND EARTH

Madison Floyd couldn't believe the audacity of the man. Lincoln Goddamn Ellison strikes again.

'Too much money in that man's pockets, if you ask me,' her friend PJ said as he swigged his beer.

'Is there such a thing?' Madison replied as she glanced away from the scene unfolding before them. Lincoln Ellison was on site at the airfield yet again to spruik one of his ambitious projects. Spaceward Bound was already launching rockets to mine asteroids. Her colleague O'Neill was heading up the first expedition. Not for her though. She'd stick to pilot training. And now what? The Moon? He was putting in a bid for the Olympus Project? That man was nuts. Spaceward Bound had no world design experience.

But he'd push his team to deliver whatever he wanted – including Madison training his girlfriend as a pilot. And, like a chump, she'd said yes. No-one says no to Lincoln Ellison.

CHAPTER 8

THE ELDER AND THE TYRANT

The Elder is the one archetype to rule them all. When embracing this archetype, we balance compassion and wisdom – the best of the heart and the best of the mind. We make sensitive and sensible decisions. Even so, hubris and the traps of power can see us in the thralls of the Tyrant, the Elder's shadow.

From a leadership maturity point of view, you might see this archetype come into use during the Achiever stage, as you start to manage teams. Emerging leaders often want to be exemplary models, and so the Elder is a good template. As a model, it also endures as you move through the next stages of Individualist and Strategist, and onwards. However, that means the shadow archetype can show up there too. Thus we see Tyrants in both new leaders and seasoned ones alike.

In the previous chapter, I looked at how you might prevent yourself from sliding into shadow to become a Tyrant. Now I outline how you might handle a Tyrant, using Conch and Coin to douse the shadow.

Reining in Tyrant Power Games

Let's run through some of the common Power Games played by Tyrants, and the counter moves you can use to neutralise them.

Power Game: Dismissiveness

The Tyrant behaves as if they have the ultimate say in all decisions, justifying it with their experience. They override others, assuming they know best due to their tenure, and dismiss contributions that challenge their authority. Nothing like being dismissed by a tyrant. Ugh.

Cause: Entitlement from experience

Having accumulated years of experience and wisdom, an individual might begin to feel entitled to deference and control. This sense of entitlement can lead to dismissing others' input and monopolising decision-making.

Counter moves

- *Frame feedback in terms of shared values:* Gently remind them of the principles they have always stood for, such as collaboration and inclusivity, to appeal to their sense of identity.

- *Ask for input as a way of empowering them:* Pose questions like, 'What advice would you give to someone else in this situation?' This reframes their authority in a helpful way and opens them up to input.

Power Game: Ruthlessness

The Tyrant uses data and logic to justify decisions, ignoring emotional or ethical considerations. They reduce people to numbers and outcomes, making decisions that may be efficient but lack compassion. This cold approach alienates others and undermines trust. Here the Tyrant thrives as the Grim Reaper, all in the name of efficiency and productivity. Yay.

Cause: Erosion of empathy

As an Elder gains power, they can become distanced from the emotional realities of others, leading to a loss of empathy. Over time, they might make decisions solely from a detached, logical perspective, without considering human impact.

Counter moves

- *Share stories:* Provide personal accounts or case studies that illustrate the human side of the issue. Appeal to their compassionate side by bringing real-world consequences into the conversation.
- *Use empathetic questioning:* Ask, 'How do you think this decision will impact morale or wellbeing?' This can guide them back to considering the people behind the data.

Power Game: Infallibility

The Tyrant behaves as if their wisdom is infallible and begins to make decisions without consulting others. They may use their perceived superiority to act as the sole source of truth, expecting unquestioning obedience. This can be amazing to see in action – more amazing still is how hard it is to confront them.

Cause: Isolation in leadership

In a position of high authority, the Elder may become isolated from genuine feedback. With fewer people willing to challenge them, they can become insulated from differing perspectives, reinforcing beliefs and slipping into the Tyrant mindset.

Counter moves

- *Frame suggestions as compliments:* Rather than challenging them directly, say things like, 'Your wisdom here is invaluable – what if we also considered …?' This approach can help them integrate new ideas without feeling undermined.
- *Bring in external expertise:* Invite external voices to consult or provide insights. By positioning these external views as contributions to the leader's wisdom, you help them remain open to broader perspectives.

Power Game: Centralising decisions, autocracy

The Tyrant consolidates power by centralising all decisions. They may veto initiatives that don't align with their vision, stifle innovation and enforce rigid hierarchies, believing that only their control can ensure success. This centralisation is sneaky and happens bit by bit, often with the collusion of others who anticipate the benefits of being a sycophant.

Cause: Fear of losing control

The Elder might become so invested in maintaining stability and control that they resist new ideas or change. This fear of losing control can cause the drift into the Tyrant shadow side, and lead to authoritarian measures to preserve their influence – that, and the heady intoxicating effect of power itself.

Counter moves

- *Build coalitions:* Work collectively with other team members to voice concerns. Present feedback as a united front, demonstrating that decentralised decision-making strengthens the team's performance.
- *Use a feedback loop:* Offer feedback gradually, over time, rather than all at once. Make suggestions during less pressured moments, which allows the Elder/Tyrant to absorb the message without feeling immediately challenged.

Power Game: Grandiose visions

The Tyrant becomes fixated on creating their legacy, demanding absolute control over the direction of projects or the organisation. They may dismiss alternative ideas as distractions from their grand vision, imposing their personal legacy at the expense of the organisation's future.

Cause: Desire for legacy preservation

The Elder, motivated by a desire to leave a lasting legacy, might start imposing their will to ensure their vision is realised. This can lead to an obsession with shaping the future in their image, ignoring the contributions of others. Expect statues and larger than life portraits at this point.

Counter moves

- *Frame legacy in terms of succession:* Appeal to the Elder's desire for a lasting impact by emphasising the importance of developing future leaders. Say something like, 'The most meaningful legacy is one that lives through others'.

- *Offer to co-create:* Present new ideas as opportunities to build something together, rather than as deviations from the Elder's vision. This helps them feel that they're still shaping the future, but with collective input.

Power Game: Micromanagement

In an attempt to control quality and outcomes and ensure no threats to their own Coin, Elders become micromanagers, and slip into the shadow of the Tyrant. They impose harsh demands, focus on productivity over people and refuse to delegate, leading to a stifling environment. To make things worse, in trying to control everything, the Tyrant may become overburdened and burned out.

Cause: Desire to control and protect their own reputation

The Elder, worried about their own reputation, defaults to extreme control. This is exhausting. In this state, they may lose patience or empathy, defaulting to authoritarian tactics simply to manage the load. It's sad to see and difficult to shift.

Counter moves

- *Offer to share the load:* Step in with practical support. Offer to take on specific tasks or decisions, positioning your offer as a way to support them rather than questioning their capability. Using phrases like, 'I can handle this piece for you', can allow you to ease the burden without triggering defensiveness.

- *Encourage the Elder/Tyrant to rest:* Remind them gently of the value of rest. Use phrases like, 'We need you at your best, and taking a step back now will help you recharge for what's ahead', to reframe rest as strategic rather than as a weakness.

- *Position delegation as a leadership strength:* Reassure them that delegating tasks isn't a sign of weakness, but a sign of wise leadership. Suggest that spreading responsibility across the team increases overall effectiveness, while ensuring their wisdom is preserved for the most critical decisions.

- *Create structures for shared leadership:* Encourage the Elder to develop processes where others can take the lead on smaller tasks or decisions, to prove capability and ease the Elder's paranoid clinging to control.

Power Game: Control and hero complex

The Tyrant becomes controlling out of a pessimistic belief that no-one else can be trusted to do the job right. They impose excessive oversight and restrict decision-making power, convinced that others are incapable or unworthy of autonomy.

Cause: Ego inflation

The success and respect that come with being an Elder may inflate the leader's ego, making them believe they are above reproach. This inflated ego can cause them to act with arrogance, believing they deserve special treatment.

Counter moves

- *Gently challenge inflated behaviour:* Frame feedback in a way that helps them see the value of humility. Say things like, 'Your leadership has really inspired collaboration among us – imagine what else we could achieve together'. This encourages humility without confrontation.

- *Recognise the team's contributions in their presence:* Publicly acknowledge the efforts of others in front of them, ensuring that the spotlight is shared. This creates an environment where ego-driven behaviour becomes less acceptable because the culture reinforces collective success.

- *Build a culture of peer feedback:* Create a system where feedback is regularly shared at all levels, including from peers to leaders. This keeps the Elder grounded and prevents ego from escalating unchecked.

- *Provide feedback in real-time:* When you see the Elder acting from a place of ego, gently offer real-time feedback. For example, 'I noticed you took the lead in the last meeting, but we missed hearing from x – perhaps next time we could balance the voices more?'

Power Game: Loyalty and punishment

The Tyrant demands recognition and deference, positioning themselves as the central figure in the organisation. They may play Power Games by rewarding loyalty to themselves rather than to the organisation, and punish those who question their authority. This is also where playing favourites rears its ugly head.

The Elder-Tyrant may divide people into loyalists and traitors rather than seeing legitimate disagreements. This binary thinking leads to favouritism (rewarding loyal followers) and harsh punishment.

Cause: Fear of irrelevance

When power is built on wisdom and longevity, the Elder may fear becoming obsolete in a changing world. This insecurity makes them double down on demanding loyalty and punishing dissenters.

Counter moves

If the Tyrant boss plays favourites, here are three counter-moves to level the playing field without becoming a target:

- *Make performance the currency, not personal favour:* Push for transparent, objective performance metrics – clear KPIs, structured promotions and documented decision-making. You might say something like, 'Can we create a standardised framework for leadership promotions to ensure we're rewarding the behaviours that reflect our values?' This makes it harder for the leader to grant favours to their sycophants.

- *Neutralise the inner circle by widening influence:* Expand cross-departmental collaboration, creating alternative power networks. Building alliances with external stakeholders, board members or clients who respect results, not loyalty, make the favourites less relevant.

- *Expose inefficiencies without confrontation:* Favourites often get away with poor decisions because no-one challenges the outcomes, only the unfairness.

By asking data-driven questions that highlight gaps in performance or decision-making, we can focus accountability without directly attacking the favourites. Consider saying something like, 'Can we review the impact of recent leadership decisions to ensure we're getting the best outcomes?' Everyone saves face and the issues get addressed.

***

The shift from Elder to its Tyrant shadow is often triggered by entitlement, fear of losing control, isolation or an inflated ego. The Tyrant plays Power Games such as monopolising decision-making, reducing people to mere numbers, imposing their will to shape their legacy and micromanaging to maintain control. These behaviours not only erode trust but also stifle creativity and collaboration, transforming the wise Elder into a domineering force. The key to maintaining the Elder's balance is for them to remain connected to empathy, collaboration and the collective wisdom of others.

Challenging a Tyrant is easier said than done. Since the Tyrant wears the Crown, they have plenty of opportunity for retribution if they are not thrilled by your well-meaning suggestions and interventions. Beware and be mindful of real consequences. Dealing with a tyrant is best done with a cohort of peers – and alliances matter here. Also remember to document everything. Steps taken here might move from gently guiding your Tyrant back to the light and helping them reclaim their Elder archetype, through to deposing a power-mongering destructive entity using whistleblower moves. This is not for the faint of heart. Know what the stakes are before you step bravely into your realignment campaign.

FEEDBACK RULES

Claire waited for the trainee at the Gaia Enterprises headquarters, in the central training room. She sat in Maja's chair behind a small stylish teak desk and mustered her anger for the confrontation.

When Julian arrived, he hesitated and looked around the spacious empty room. The air-conditioning kicked up a level as the oppressive midday sun blasted the windows. He walked slowly over to Claire and stood before her. There was no chair for him.

'Julian, it has come to my attention that you have issues with the way our training is being delivered here.' Clare stared hard at her quarry.

'I beg your pardon?' he said, confused. He put his hands in his back pockets and rocked on his toes, eyebrows furrowed.

'Many have told me that you think the training regime is outdated and the scoring mechanisms are too pedantic.' Clare tapped a finger on the desk for emphasis.

'That's not true—'

'I'll have you know that the training program has had a decade of development, with the most rigorous of oversight and continuous review. It has garnered international acclaim and is the envy of all other world designers.'

Julian's cheeks bloomed red and he bit his lip.

Claire clasped her hands on the desk as she had often seen Maja do and held Julian's gaze until he looked away, face burning.

A lazy fly droned past them and butted the window with a sluggish thud ... thud ... thud. It buzzed to a stop on the window ledge and considered its options for escape before launching towards the door behind Julian.

Clare remained silent until he looked back at her, sheepish.

'If you have issues with the training program, you are to come directly to me. At Gaia, we value speaking the truth. If you don't feel comfortable with that, other agencies, like Spaceward Bound, will gladly accept two-faced weasels. Is that clear?'

CHAPTER 9

THE WARRIOR AND THE BULLY

The Warrior fights for rights. When we embody the Warrior, we stand firm in our focus to protect others and advocate for their rights and dignity. If we get too fixated on our perspective, however, we may slide into the shadow of this archetype – the Bully.

The Bully is an intimidating figure. They use their propensity for arguing, and being forceful and focused – admirable qualities in a Warrior – to full effect to get their way and oppress others. It is not nice.

First things first

In this chapter, I outline some ways to reduce a Bully's power in your workplace. Before trying out these options, however, keep in mind the following important considerations:

- *Safety first:* If you feel threatened or unsafe, prioritise your wellbeing and remove yourself from the situation.
- *Workplace culture:* Consider how your workplace typically handles conflict. This can influence your approach.
- *Confidence:* Even if you don't feel confident, try to project a calm and assertive demeanour. This can sometimes deter a Bully.
- *Support network:* Talk to trusted colleagues, friends or family. See if they've witnessed similar behaviour. Having a support system can make a big difference.

- *Document everything and keep detailed records:* Record every incident, date, time, what was said/done and any witnesses. This is crucial if you need to escalate the issue. Also save emails and other messages, because any written evidence of bullying is valuable.

- *Pick your battles:* Sometimes, it's best to let minor comments slide rather than engaging in a confrontation.

And remember:

- *It's not your fault:* You are not responsible for someone else's bullying behaviour.

- *You have rights:* You have the right to a safe and respectful workplace.

- *Don't suffer in silence:* Addressing bullying is crucial for your wellbeing and career.

Tackling a Bully

Here are some of the common Power Games played by Bullies, and the counter moves you can use to neutralise them.

Power Game: Domination

The Bully uses intimidation and fear to enforce their will, dominating others by projecting strength and using threats, whether implicit or explicit.

Cause: Fear of losing control

The Bully feels a need to maintain control over people or situations, and resorts to intimidation to assert dominance. This often stems from insecurity or fear of appearing weak. This behaviour may also stem from lingering issues at the Expert stage of leadership maturity, where status needs to be consolidated and recognised. Dominating others is a twisted way to demonstrate one-upmanship.

Counter moves:

- *Consider first of all any threats to physical safety:* Counter moves are also best done with witnesses.

- *Be direct and assertive (if you feel safe and comfortable):*
  – 'That's not appropriate.' A clear statement showing you won't tolerate disrespect.
  – 'I don't appreciate the way you're speaking to me.' This highlights their behaviour is the issue.
  – 'Please stop *[specific behaviour]*. It's making me uncomfortable.' Be direct about what needs to change.
  – 'I'm happy to discuss this professionally, but I won't tolerate personal attacks.' This sets a boundary for respectful communication.

- *Escalate the situation:* If direct communication with the Bully fails, involve someone in authority such as your supervisor or manager in HR. Present your documented evidence when talking with this person.

- *Know your company's policies:* Many workplaces have policies against bullying and harassment. Familiarise yourself with them.

- *Consider external options:* If internal channels don't help, consult with a lawyer or labour rights organisation.

Power Game: Controls the conversation

The Bully often dominates conversations, shutting down differing opinions by monopolising the dialogue and invalidating others' perspectives.

Cause: Desire to be heard and respected

The Bully may believe their perspective is the only correct one and so dominates conversations to ensure their ideas prevail. This is often driven by a deep-seated need for validation and respect.

Counter moves

- *Gentle interruptions:*
    - 'I understand your point, and I'd like to add …' Acknowledge their perspective while creating space for yours.
    - 'That's an interesting perspective. Before we move on, could I just mention …' Politely redirect the flow.
    - 'Hold on a moment, I think *[colleague's name]* had something to say earlier.' Bring others back into the conversation.

- *Refocus the discussion:*
    - 'That's a good point, yet how does that relate to *[the main topic]*?' Gently steer the conversation back on track.
    - 'Can we hear from others on this? I'm interested in different perspectives.' Encourage broader participation.
    - 'Perhaps we can discuss that separately later. For now, let's focus on …' Table their tangent for another time.

- *Validate others:*
    - 'I see what you're saying, and I think *[colleague's name]* brought up a valid point, too.' Acknowledge different viewpoints.
    - 'It's important to consider all sides of this issue before making a decision.' Emphasise the value of diverse opinions.

- *Protect your time:*
    - 'I'm on a tight deadline, so I can only stay for another *[time limit]*. Can we make sure to hear from everyone quickly?' Set a boundary.
    - 'I have another meeting soon, but I'd like to hear more about this later.' Politely exit the conversation.

Power Game: Coercion

Bullies can use their position or role to coerce others into compliance, forcing outcomes through threats of consequences or by wielding disproportionate control.

Cause: Need for compliance

Bullies who coerce others often have a rigid view of how things should be done and feel threatened when others don't conform. They manipulate through threats to force alignment with their vision, fearing loss of order or authority. Dealing with this can be tricky, especially when you lack the authority to challenge them directly.

Counter moves

- *Appeal to reason and policy:*
  - 'I understand you want *[outcome]*. I'm unclear if this approach is in line with company policy.' Subtly remind them of the rules.
  - 'I'm concerned that this might create a hostile work environment. Could we explore alternative solutions?' Highlight the potential consequences of their actions.
  - 'I'm willing to cooperate. I would like to understand how this decision was made and why it's necessary.' Request justification and transparency.
- *Talk to colleagues:* If others are experiencing similar coercion, consider addressing the issue as a group. Remember – strength increases with numbers.
- *Seek support from a trusted colleague:* Even if they can't directly intervene, having someone to confide in can make a difference.
- *Escalate if necessary:* If direct communication and other tactics fail, consider escalating the issue to someone in HR with more authority. Present your documented evidence when talking with this person.

- *Know your rights:* Familiarise yourself with your company's policies on workplace conduct and any relevant labour laws.

- *Protect yourself:* Don't give in to unreasonable demands. Stand your ground, even if it's uncomfortable.

- *Set boundaries:* Politely and firmly refuse to engage in discussions or tasks that are outside your job description or make you feel uncomfortable.

- *Prioritise your wellbeing:* Coercive behaviour can take a toll on your mental health. Seek support from friends or family, or a therapist if needed.

Power Game: Belittling

A Bully belittles others, often using mockery, sarcasm or passive-aggressive remarks to diminish someone's worth or contributions. This behaviour feels so immature, and yet is desperately cutting when you're on the receiving end.

Cause: Insecurity and self-doubt

The Bully belittler often projects their own insecurities onto others, using mockery or sarcasm to diminish others' confidence. By making others feel small, they temporarily feel more powerful.

Counter moves

- *Call them out (if you feel safe):*

    - 'That's a belittling comment. Could you rephrase that?' Directly address the behaviour and ask for a more respectful approach.

    - 'I'm not sure what you mean by that. Can you clarify without the sarcasm?' Force them to be more explicit and less passive-aggressive.

    - 'I appreciate constructive feedback. This feels more like a personal attack.' Draw a line between helpful criticism and hurtful comments.

- *Deflect and redirect:*
    - *[In response to a sarcastic remark]* 'I'm glad you find that amusing.' A neutral response such as this doesn't engage with the negativity.
    - 'I'm focused on *[the task/goal]* right now. Can we keep our comments relevant to that?' Shift the focus back to the work at hand.
    - 'I'm happy to discuss this further if you can approach it with respect.' Set a boundary for how you expect to be treated.
- *Focus on your own value and don't internalise their negativity:* Remember that their behaviour is a reflection of them, not you.
- *Affirm your strengths:* Remind yourself of your skills and accomplishments.
- *Seek support outside of work:* Talk to friends, family or a therapist to help you process your emotions and maintain your self-esteem.

Power Game: Steamrolling

The Bully overpowers others through sheer force of will, using aggressive tactics to 'win' at all costs, often dismissing or trampling over nuanced discussions or solutions. When the Bully bundles this with anger and frustration, it is truly intimidating.

Cause: Obsession with winning

The Bully becomes fixated on winning or being 'right' at all costs. They lose sight of collaboration and believe overpowering others is the quickest way to achieve their goals. This behaviour is often fuelled by a competitive mindset or ego.

Counter moves

- *Stand your ground (calmly):*
  - 'I understand your passion, and I think we need to consider other perspectives before making a decision.' Acknowledge their intensity while advocating for a more inclusive approach.
  - 'I hear what you're saying, and I disagree with *[specific point]*. Here's why ...' Don't be afraid to disagree respectfully and offer your reasoning.
  - 'It seems like we're talking over each other. Can we take turns sharing our thoughts?' Try to establish a more structured and less combative communication style.

- *Appeal to collaboration and reason:*
  - 'Our goal is to find the best solution for everyone, not just 'win' the argument. Can we work together on this?' Reframe the situation as a collaborative effort, not a competition.
  - 'I think a compromise is possible here that we haven't explored yet. What if we ...' Suggest alternative solutions that address multiple needs.
  - 'I'm concerned that this approach might have unintended consequences. Have we considered ...?' Raise potential issues to encourage more thoughtful consideration.

- *Shift the focus:*
  - 'Can we take a step back and look at the bigger picture here?' Encourage a broader perspective beyond immediate 'wins'.
  - 'Let's focus on the data and the facts. What does the evidence suggest?' Ground the discussion in objective information to reduce emotional arguments.
  - 'Perhaps we can break this down into smaller steps. What's the most important issue to address first?' Make the

problem seem less overwhelming and encourage a more methodical approach.

- *Protect yourself and don't get drawn into their aggression:* Stay calm and composed, even if they're raising their voice or being dismissive.

Power Game: Agitation

The Bully might rile up a group by appealing to emotion, fear or anger to create mob-like behaviour or groupthink, using the power of numbers to intimidate others into submission. Fun times.

Cause: Fear of being challenged alone

The Bully manipulates crowds to hide behind groupthink because they fear standing alone or being directly challenged. By riling up others, they gain strength in numbers and shift the pressure away from themselves.

Counter moves

- *Stay calm and rational, rather than getting caught up in the emotional frenzy:* The Bully agitator wants to create chaos and bypass logical discussion. Maintain your composure and don't react impulsively.

- *Appeal to reason and logic:* Say something like, 'I understand people are feeling strongly about this, and can we take a step back and look at the facts?' or 'While emotions are important, we need to base our decisions on evidence and sound reasoning'.

- *Challenge the narrative:* Question the Bully's assumptions and generalisations with something like, 'Is it fair to say that everyone feels this way?' or 'Should we consider other perspectives before jumping to conclusions?'

- *Point out the dangers of groupthink:* 'It's important that we hear diverse viewpoints and avoid making hasty decisions based on pressure.'

- *Highlight the potential consequences of their actions:* 'If we let fear and anger dictate our actions, we risk making decisions we'll regret later.'
- *Encourage quieter voices to speak up:* 'I'd be interested in hearing what [colleague's name] thinks about this.'
- *Validate dissenting opinions:* 'That's a valid point, and it's important that we consider all sides of this issue.'
- *Show solidarity with those being targeted:* 'I don't agree with the way [colleague's name] is being treated. We need to foster a more respectful environment.'
- *Shift the focus by redirecting the conversation to facts and data:* 'Can we look at the evidence before making any decisions?'
- *Propose a structured decision-making process:* 'Perhaps we can use a more formal method to evaluate the options and ensure everyone's voice is heard.'
- *Suggest a break or time-out:* 'It seems like emotions are running high. Maybe we should take a break and come back to this later with fresh perspectives.'
- *Protect yourself by not engaging in personal attacks or insults:* Stay focused on the issue at hand and avoid getting drawn into a shouting match.

Power Game: Moral grandstanding

Bullies frame themselves as morally superior, weaponising their sense of righteousness to shame or guilt others into compliance, often closing down debate by claiming the ethical high ground. The smell of sanctimoniousness is sickening. Gag.

Cause: Self-righteousness or guilt avoidance

This Bully feels the need to assert moral superiority to justify their actions or avoid confronting their own shortcomings. By shaming others, they distract from any ethical ambiguity in their own behaviour and reinforce their self-image as 'the good one'.

Counter moves

- *Separate the issue from the person by focusing on the facts and logic:* 'I understand your concerns. Can we discuss the practical implications of this decision?' or 'While ethical considerations are important, we also need to consider the data and evidence'.

- *Avoid getting drawn into moral debates:* 'I respect your values, and I have a different perspective on this issue. Can we focus on finding a solution that works for everyone?'

- *Challenge their assumptions by questioning their claims of moral superiority:* 'What makes you believe your perspective is the only ethical one?' or 'What other valid moral viewpoints should we consider?'

- *Expose any inconsistencies in their arguments:* 'You seem to be applying different standards to yourself than to others. Can you explain why?'

- *Point out the potential for self-righteousness:* 'It's important to be mindful of our own biases and avoid judging others too harshly.'

- *Appeal to shared values and find common ground:* 'I think we both agree that [shared value] is important. Can we find a solution that upholds this value?'

- *Reframe the issue in terms of shared goals:* 'We all want what's best for the company/team/project. How can we achieve that together?'

- *Emphasise the importance of collaboration and compromise:* 'No-one has a monopoly on morality. We need to work together to find a solution that respects everyone's values.'

- *Set boundaries and don't engage in guilt trips or emotional manipulation:* 'I'm not comfortable being shamed or guilted into compliance. Can we have a respectful discussion instead?'

- *Refuse to be silenced:* 'I have a right to express my opinion, even if it differs from yours.'

- *Walk away if necessary:* 'If you're not willing to have a constructive conversation, I'm going to excuse myself.'

- *Talk to colleagues:* See if others have experienced similar behaviour and are willing to support a more balanced approach. Seek advice from a trusted mentor or advisor, and ask for guidance on how to navigate this challenging personality.

- *Don't get defensive:* Getting caught up in defending your own morality is easy, but try to stay focused on the issue at hand.

- *Stay calm and respectful:* Even if the other person is being condescending or judgemental, maintain your composure.

＊＊＊

Dealing with a Bully is a scary prospect because they use threats as their modus operandi. By maintaining a calm, focused and inclusive approach, you can embody the Warrior archetype – neutralising the Bully's tactics and ensuring that power is used to uplift rather than suppress.

Finding strength to use the counter moves is easier when you have colleagues who can support you and an organisational culture that does not accept this type of behaviour. If you find yourself in a culture where bullying is tolerated, you may choose to work your way into a position where you can use the Crown (and its authority) to change culture and the systems that enable bullying. This is a long road. Keep yourself safe along the way. To change the systems, read ahead to chapters 13 and 14, where I discuss building healthy power structures in teams and in organisations.

BACK CHANNEL NEGOTIATIONS

'What do you want, Lincoln?' Aryanna's voice was cold as steel in space. She looked up from the tender documents for the Olympus Project as Lincoln swaggered in to her office with a broad smile. His pet dog, a fluffy Pomeranian called Mr Puffkins, bounded beside him and came scurrying up to Aryanna for a sniff. She glanced at the dog with disdain and then stared at Lincoln, waiting.

'I love it. Straight to the point, eh Aryanna? No messing around.' Lincoln sank into a chair across from her and grinned.

'Well?' she said, her smooth face implacable.

'Now that we're both on the Lunar commission, and both tendering for the Olympus Project, I thought we could come to some sort of arrangement.' Lincoln leaned forward with a knowing look.

Aryanna pushed the tender documents aside, and steepled her fingers. She waited for just a heartbeat. 'What did you have in mind?'

CHAPTER 10

THE DIPLOMAT AND THE MANIPULATOR

The Diplomat is the master of influence. As a Diplomat, you're focused on winning, but not in a win–lose paradigm. You stick to our values, while seeking to understand others, and you want an outcome that benefits as many as possible.

If we lose sight of our ethical core and our values compass, and become hell-bent on getting our way, we slip into the Diplomat's shadow – the Manipulator.[15] This is the most common shadow archetype we see in Power Games. Aryanna and Lincoln from the preceding scenario are both playing high-stakes diplomacy, with major projects hanging in the breeze. Such negotiations can slide into manipulation, especially when held behind closed doors. But who is manipulating who? Power Games can be tricky.

Dealing with a Manipulator

Take a deep breath, this stuff ain't fun.

Power Game: Back-channelling

Manipulators may covertly influence decisions and actions through back-channel conversations, gossip or strategically

---

[15] In *People Stuff* I named the shadow to the Diplomat the Trickster. In the context of Power Games and office politics, I felt the Manipulator a more apt name for this shadow.

planting ideas to shape outcomes without being directly involved. They are duplicitous and cunning, and leave you feeling icky all over.

Cause: Fear of losing control

When individuals feel they are losing influence or control, they may resort to manipulation to reassert dominance or regain perceived power. This often stems from insecurity or fear of being sidelined.

Counter moves

- *Remember your values and main objective:* Bring the Manipulator's actions into the open without appearing confrontational, and shift the conversation into a transparent, collaborative space.

- *Frame ideas or initiatives as being in the best interest of collective success:* Use persuasive communication to position yourself as an ally rather than as a threat. Offer solutions that align with the Manipulator's goals, subtly guiding them back to collaboration.

- *Prompt collaboration with these helpful phrases:*
    - 'I know maintaining consistency is important to you – how about we explore this new approach that can preserve control while opening up more opportunities for the team?'
    - 'I've heard a few different perspectives on this, including some important points you've raised privately. I think it would benefit everyone if we discussed these openly, so we're all aligned.'
    - 'If we can get everything on the table, it'll help us move forward together with a unified strategy.'
    - 'It's important that we surface all these ideas so we can build a stronger plan that includes everyone's input.'

Power Game: Using people for advancement

The Manipulator uses others as stepping stones, manipulating relationships, alliances or projects for ladder climbing and to advance their position, often at the expense of others' reputations or opportunities. Tactics can include flattery and sucking up. Psychopaths are particularly good at this as they weave a web of charisma and charm, only to drop you like a stone once you've served their purpose. Scoundrels.

Cause: Ambition and greed

Unchecked ambition, especially when paired with a desire for personal gain, can lead someone to manipulate situations and people. They might rationalise their behaviour as necessary to achieve success, especially if they equate power with status or material rewards.

Counter moves

- *Emphasise the importance of collective success over individual gain:* This encourages a focus on teamwork that makes it harder for the Manipulator to continue advancing by stepping on others or currying favour from those with authority.
- *Use your status (Coin) to build alliances and gather supporters:* By creating a network of allies who back your ideas, you raise your profile and make it harder for the Manipulator to act solely in their own interests.
- *Consider helpful phrases such as the following:*
  - 'I've spoken to several colleagues who share this perspective. It seems like we could all benefit if we approached this together as a team.'
  - 'I think this project would be even stronger if we could all contribute our strengths. That way, everyone benefits from the shared success.'

- 'This initiative really came together thanks to the input from the whole team, especially *[colleague's name]*, who handled the key logistics.'
- 'Let's make sure we're giving credit where it's due – there's been a lot of great work from *[team member]*.'

Power Game: Sabotage

Manipulators might sabotage competitors or colleagues by withholding critical information, undermining trust or subtly spreading doubt, creating obstacles for others while positioning themselves as the solution. It's amazing how little conscience some people have.

Cause: Desperation and scarcity thinking

When people feel desperate – whether due to personal, professional or financial pressures – they may abandon their ethical compass in favour of short-term, self-serving strategies. Scarcity thinking creates the illusion that winning can only come at the expense of others. This is the dog-eat-dog world of the Opportunist – a very early stage of leadership maturity, before even the Diplomat stage.

Counter moves

- *Create transparency and accountability while maintaining a constructive and non-confrontational tone:* If the Manipulator operates from a scarcity mindset, use your influence (Conch) to shift the narrative towards one of abundance and possibilities. Highlight opportunities and how collaboration leads to better results, reassuring them that success isn't a zero-sum game.
- *Use phrases like these as needed:*
  - 'There's plenty of opportunity for everyone if we work together on this – our combined efforts can make the outcome even stronger.'

- 'Let's document this so we're all aligned on the next steps and everyone has access to the same information.'
- 'I noticed there's been some confusion – let's bring everyone together to clarify things and make sure we're all moving forward on the same page.'
- 'Could you share that update with the team? It's important we're all aware of any changes, so no-one's caught off guard.'

Power Game: Gaslighting

Manipulators may distort reality, twist facts or subtly undermine others' confidence to keep them off balance. By questioning others' perspectives, they gain psychological leverage. This tactic is particularly dastardly because it leaves the hapless colleague steeped in self-doubt.

Cause: Personal insecurity or ego

A fragile ego or low self-esteem can drive someone to manipulate others to feel validated or indispensable. Manipulation becomes a way to mask insecurity and to present a facade of control or superiority – that, or they're a psychopath with no qualms in derailing others for their own gain.

Counter moves

- *Maintain control of the conversation, grounding it in facts and documentation, while offering a non-confrontational way to address the gaslighter's tactics:* Manipulators driven by insecurity or ego can often be neutralised by carefully using status (Coin) to offer recognition. Acknowledge their contributions publicly, but ensure it's framed in a way that supports the broader team. This lowers their need for manipulative power plays as they receive the validation they seek.
- *Helpful phrases:*
  - 'Your insights really helped shape this initiative – your experience is invaluable to our success here.'

- 'Let's clarify what was agreed on earlier, just to make sure we're all on the same page.'
- 'I remember it differently – how about we check the notes or emails to avoid any misunderstandings?'
- 'It seems like we have different perspectives on this – let's get a third opinion to help clarify.'

Power Game: Stealing credit

Manipulators position themselves to take credit for work or ideas that aren't theirs, possibly by downplaying others' contributions or positioning themselves as the face of team efforts. This is just downright affronting and brazen, but in a poor culture with little accountability, they can get away with it.

Cause: Desire for recognition or approval

The need for approval from higher-ups or external stakeholders can cause someone to manipulate outcomes to appear more competent or successful than they really are. They may tailor situations to ensure they receive credit for achievements, even if it means deceiving others.

Counter moves

- *Ensure the right people are acknowledged, without directly accusing the credit stealer or escalating tension:* If the Manipulator seeks recognition, use your influence (Conch) to create an environment where mutual credit is the norm. Publicly acknowledging others, while suggesting a team-focused approach to success, encourages a shift away from personal gain and promotes shared accomplishments.
- *Use phrases such as the following:*
  - 'It's clear we're all contributing something valuable here – let's make sure everyone's role is acknowledged as part of the bigger picture.'

- 'I'm really proud of how our team pulled this off – especially *[specific colleague's]* contribution on *[specific task]*, which made a huge difference.'
- 'It's great that this idea came together. I remember when *[colleague's name]* first suggested that approach during our last discussion – good to see it taking shape!'
- 'It's been a real group effort – let's make sure we recognise everyone's role in bringing this to life.'

Power Game: Playing all sides

In this game, the Manipulator switches allegiances opportunistically, bends rules or shifts ethical standards depending on which side benefits them the most at the moment, displaying little loyalty or integrity.

Cause: Competing values or moral flexibility

Some individuals have a flexible moral framework that allows them to rationalise manipulation when their values clash with personal ambition. This often happens when they view the ends as justifying the means.

Counter moves

- *Maintain a focus on collective goals, inclusivity and long-term thinking:* This counters the opportunist's self-serving tendencies. Use your status (Coin) to highlight the organisation's or team's core values and ethical expectations. Bring attention to shared values that the Manipulator may be compromising, and position yourself as someone aligned with the group's standards.
- *Use the following phrases as needed:*
  - 'In our team, we've always valued transparency and fairness – it's important that we continue upholding these principles as we move forward with this project.'

- 'That's an interesting angle – how does it fit into our long-term goals and the team's priorities?'
- 'Before we move forward, let's weigh the pros and cons and make sure this benefits everyone involved.'
- 'I see the potential in this. Let's involve the rest of the team to get their perspectives and make sure it's the right direction.'

Power Game: Bribes and favours

Manipulators work behind the scenes, influencing outcomes through invisible networks or relationships, often evading accountability because their actions are difficult to trace.

Cause: Lack of accountability or oversight

In environments where accountability is weak, individuals may feel they can manipulate without consequence. This lack of checks and balances emboldens them to engage in covert tactics to achieve their goals.

Counter moves

- *Promote transparency and accountability without directly calling out the shadow player, making it harder for them to operate in secrecy:* If the Manipulator operates due to a lack of accountability, use your influence (Conch) to advocate for more transparent processes. By championing clarity and openness in decision-making, you can create a culture that makes manipulation difficult to sustain.
- *Consider the following helpful phrases:*
    - 'To make sure we're all on the same page, could we document these decisions so everyone has a clear understanding of the process?'
    - 'It would be great to get everyone's input on this – let's make sure we're all aligned and clear on the next steps.'

- 'I've heard a few different viewpoints on this – how about we clarify everything in the next meeting so we all have the same information?'
- 'Just to make sure nothing gets missed, could we document key decisions and share them with the team?'

Power Game: Fake friendships

Here, the Manipulator feigns vulnerability or understanding to manipulate emotions and gain trust, only to exploit that trust for personal or strategic advantage. This is also a common tactic of the psychopath.

Cause: Emotional manipulation or leverage

People who are highly skilled in reading and leveraging emotions may use their understanding of others' psychological states to manipulate outcomes. Emotional manipulation can be especially potent in power dynamics, because it preys on vulnerabilities.

Counter moves

- *Maintain empathy while setting boundaries and keeping the focus on team-oriented solutions, making it harder for the empathy exploiter to manipulate emotions for personal gain:* Manipulators who exploit emotions can be countered by reinforcing emotional boundaries. Use your status (Coin) to model emotionally intelligent behaviour and encourage others to set healthy boundaries, making it clear that emotional manipulation won't succeed.

- *Helpful phrases:*
  - 'It's important we stay focused on the facts and not let emotions cloud our judgment – let's ensure we're making decisions based on the data and clear goals.'
  - 'I understand this is a difficult situation – let's focus on finding a solution that works for everyone.'

- 'It's important we consider everyone's perspective and keep things balanced – how can we ensure this decision is fair to the whole team?'

- 'I hear you, and I'm sure others feel the same way. How can we move forward together while keeping our goals in mind?'

Power Game: Playing the victim

All sorts of 'fun' things come out here. The Manipulator stirs up drama to put themselves at the centre of the conversation, with an overall theme of being hard done by. It's a type of emotional coercion.

Cause: Playing on sympathies

This type of behaviour may stem from past hurt or trauma, perhaps worthy of sympathy and compassion. Nonetheless, capitulating to their wishes only further anchors them in this passive-aggressive Power Game.

Counter moves

- *Challenge language and assumptions:* Often, playing the victim will entail the Manipulator using absolutes such as 'you always ...' and 'you never ...'. This is a great opportunity to pick up on these extremes to dial back the rhetoric. They might also use phrases like, 'you made me feel ...', 'I have to speak my truth' and 'I'm being silenced/ignored/sidelined/bullied/shut down' (when they are not).

- *Keep the conversation focused on solutions rather than reacting to the accusations with these helpful phrases:*

    - 'What would you like instead?'

    - 'What systems or processes do you suggest to keep this from happening?'

    - 'What are some alternatives to this situation?'

- 'What does a positive resolution look like to you that respects all parties?'

Power Game: Toxic gossip

Instead of challenging and questioning, Manipulators seed misinformation and malignant stories.

Cause: Shoring up support

Jealousy and insecurity can lead to manipulation in the shadows. By building up factions and divisions, Manipulators shore up a power base that can cut down a more stalwart individual who might have no problem naming the Manipulator's faulty logic, ineptitude or poor intentions.

Counter moves

- *Implement transparent team processes and positive norms around constructive conflict:* This can help neutralise this type of manipulation. Where these processes and norms are absent, you can shut down the overtures of toxic gossip directly, thereby establishing a boundary and an ethical stand.

- *Helpful phrases:*
    - When they say, 'I shouldn't be sharing this, but ...' say, 'I'm glad you identified something that should remain confidential. It can be tempting to share. How can I help you keep it to yourself?'
    - When they say, 'This is supposed to be confidential, but ...' say, 'Thanks. Let's keep it that way. I know it's tempting to share, but let's honour the right intention.'
    - When they say, 'You wouldn't believe this about *[colleague's name]*. I just heard ...' say, 'Wait, am I the right person to be telling this to? Maybe you should talk to HR if it's a big concern for you?'

***

The key to countering these power plays is fostering self-awareness, accountability and ethical grounding, ensuring that influence is wielded for the greater good, as the Diplomat would do, rather than for selfish gain.

From a leadership maturity point of view, use of manipulation for personal gain is symptomatic of the Opportunist (pre-Diplomat) stage of development, where we feel it is us against the world. It's eat or be eaten. A longer term strategy is to help the individual value working in a team and being part of a group. This is the shift towards the Diplomat stage of leadership maturity, and requires emphasising belonging, team identity and cohesion, supporting one other, and strength in teamwork.

If you're dealing with a psychopath, and four in 100 are such types, then all of that is moot. You need to activate a 'contain and neutralise' campaign instead, using some of the strategies listed in this chapter.

The Manipulator is a slippery fish. These kinds of Power Games can you leave you reeling, questioning your faith in humanity and your own competency as a professional. I have had many conversations with leaders who have been left bruised and wounded by Manipulators. With some of these tools in your toolkit, you may be better equipped to push back and contain their corrosive behaviour.

LEGACY OR LANGUISH

'Maja, I really think you need to reconsider,' Claire said. She walked alongside her mentor as they toured the Gaia Headquarters. 'Do we really want to throw our hat in the ring with all those space cowboys? Think of our legacy, our mission – it's all about Earth, not space.'

Maja sighed. 'Claire, we have been through this many times. Aryanna is our primary funder now and so we have an obligation to consider her interests, as well as the financial reality of Gaia Enterprises.'

'But we're steering off course, Maja!' Claire grabbed Maja's arm and slowed so her mentor would look her in the face. 'We're selling out our values for corporate ambition!'

Maja smiled gently. 'Claire, if we don't expand our services, we will have no future. This is not a black and white issue.'

'Isn't it?' Claire asked, perplexed. 'It's Earth or space. Pretty clear really.'

'It's Earth *and* space. And the new direction can support our legacy. You'll see.'

'I don't think so,' muttered Claire.

CHAPTER 11

THE GUARDIAN AND THE FANATIC

When we take on the role of the Guardian, we are looking to protect what's best about an organisation, team or process, while still moving forward. We caution throwing all the good things away in the name of progress. If we get too attached to our perspective – and start to exclude all others who don't agree with us – we can devolve into the Fanatic shadow archetype, and our Conch loses influence.

Restraining a Fanatic

Dealing with a Fanatic requires patience and finesse. Here we go.

Power Game: Stonewalling

The Fanatic blocks new ideas or changes by constantly referencing the past, positioning themselves as the sole protector of the organisation's heritage. They may withhold approvals, drag out processes or overemphasise risks to stall progress.

Cause: Fear of losing legacy

The Fanatic might fear that the values, traditions or systems they are protecting will be completely erased by progress. This attachment to legacy can cloud their judgement, pushing them to extreme measures to preserve the past. They may use old tattered phrases such as, 'But we've always done it this way' or, 'Back in my day …' Cue rolling of the eyes. But that doesn't help when the Fanatic steps up their campaign.

Counter moves

- *Acknowledge and respect the past:*
    - 'I understand you've been with the company for a long time and have valuable insights into its history.' Show appreciation for their knowledge and experience.
    - 'I appreciate the role that tradition has played in our success, and I want to ensure we respect that as we move forward.' Acknowledge the importance of tradition.
    - 'I think we both agree that *[shared value or past achievement]* is something to be proud of. How can we build on that foundation?' Find common ground.

- *Focus on the future and its benefits:*
    - 'This new approach aligns with our core values of innovation and customer satisfaction.' Connect new ideas to the organisation's established mission and values.
    - 'By embracing this new technology, we can improve efficiency, reduce costs and reach new markets.' Highlight the potential benefits of change.
    - 'Imagine if we could achieve *[positive outcome]* by implementing this change. It would be a significant step forward for our organisation.' Paint a compelling vision of the future.

- *Address concerns and risks:*
    - 'I understand your concerns about the risks involved. Here's how we plan to mitigate them …' Acknowledge the Fanatic's concerns and address them directly.
    - 'Research shows that this new approach has been successful in other organisations.' Provide data and evidence to support your arguments.

- 'We can address your concerns about *[specific issue]* by implementing *[solution]*.' Offer solutions to potential challenges.

- *Build a coalition for change:*
    - 'I've been discussing this with *[colleague's name]*, and they're also excited about the potential benefits.' Enlist the support of colleagues who are open to new ideas.
    - 'A growing number of us believe that this change is necessary for our organisation to thrive.' Present a united front.
    - If possible, find someone with authority (perhaps in a higher position) who is receptive to your ideas and can help champion them as an ally.

- *Be patient and persistent:*
    - 'I'd like to revisit this proposal and share some new information that might address your concerns.' Continue to present your ideas in a clear and compelling way.
    - Don't expect to change the Fanatic's mind overnight. It may take time and repeated efforts to persuade them.
    - Don't give up – even if they resist initially, they may eventually come around if you demonstrate the value of your ideas.

- *Important considerations:*
    - Respect their position. Even if you disagree with their approach, acknowledge their role in the organisation.
    - Be prepared for resistance. Change is often met with scepticism, especially from those who are attached to the past.
    - Document your efforts by keeping a record of your conversations and any roadblocks you encounter.

Power Game: Defensiveness

The Fanatic plays a defensive game, seeing any new idea or process as a personal affront. They might reject changes out of hand, justify outdated practices or create barriers to innovation, believing that only their approach is valid.

Cause: Over-identification with their role

When the Fanatic becomes too identified with their role as the protector of certain values or processes, they may feel personally threatened by change, seeing it as an attack on their identity or contribution.

Counter moves:

- *Emphasise collaboration and shared goals:*
  - 'I value your expertise and want to work with you to make things even better.' Position yourself as an ally, not an adversary.
  - 'We both want what's best for the team/company, right? Let's explore how this idea could contribute to that.' Frame the new idea as a way to achieve shared objectives.
  - 'I know you've had success with the current approach, and I want to build on that success with this new idea.' Acknowledge their past achievements while suggesting improvement.

- *Validate their concerns and expertise:*
  - 'I understand your hesitation. Change can be challenging. What are your specific concerns about this new idea?' Actively listen to their objections and show that you value their input.
  - 'You've clearly mastered the current system. Can you help us understand how this new idea might impact it?' Leverage their expertise to analyse the potential effects of the change.

- 'Your experience is invaluable. Can you help us anticipate any challenges and find solutions?' Make them feel like a vital part of the process.

- *Focus on data and evidence:*
  - 'I've done some research, and the data suggests that this new approach could lead to *[positive outcomes]*.' Back up your suggestions with objective information.
  - 'Other companies have successfully implemented this idea and seen significant improvements in *[areas of concern]*.' Provide examples and case studies to demonstrate the effectiveness of the new approach.
  - 'Let's run a small pilot project to test this idea and gather data before making a full-scale change.' Suggest a low-risk way to evaluate the new approach.

- *Appeal to their sense of ownership:*
  - 'I'd love to get your feedback on how we can refine this idea and make it even better.' Involve them in the process of shaping the change.
  - 'This new approach could give you more control over *[area of responsibility]* and free up your time for *[more fulfilling tasks]*.' Highlight the potential benefits for them personally.
  - 'With your expertise, you could be a key player in leading this change and ensuring its success.' Appeal to their desire for recognition and influence.

- *Be patient and persistent:*
  - 'I wanted to follow up on our conversation and see if you have any further thoughts or questions.' Continue to address their concerns and provide support.
  - Don't expect immediate buy-in. It may take time and multiple conversations to win them over.

The Guardian and the Fanatic

- Celebrate small victories and acknowledge any progress made. This shows appreciation for their willingness to consider new ideas.

- *Important considerations:*
  - Avoid confrontation and don't directly challenge their defensiveness. Instead, focus on building trust and collaboration.
  - Be respectful and empathetic. Acknowledge that change can be difficult and understand their perspective.
  - Again, document your efforts and keep a record of your conversations and any roadblocks you encounter.

Power Game: Righteousness

The Fanatic can assume the role of arbiter, declaring certain ideas as 'right' or 'wrong' without considering nuance. They may dismiss compromise or collaboration, framing their stance as the only ethical or viable option.

Cause: Overconfidence in their perspective

When the Fanatic becomes too confident in their judgement, they may discount other viewpoints, believing that they alone understand what's best. This overconfidence can make them inflexible and unpleasant to work with.

Counter moves:

- *Appeal to shared values and goals:*
  - 'I understand you're passionate about *[their cause/value]*. I think we both agree that *[shared value or goal]* is important. Can we find a solution that honours both?' Find common ground.
  - 'While it's important to uphold our values, we also need to achieve *[desired outcome]*. How can we do that in a way that aligns with our shared principles?' Shift the focus to outcomes.

- 'We're all on the same team, and we need to work together to achieve our goals. Can we find a way to bridge our differences and move forward together?' Emphasise the importance of unity and collaboration.

- *Challenge their assumptions (respectfully):*
  - 'I respect your perspective, and is it possible that other viewpoints or solutions are also valid?' Question their claim to absolute truth.
  - 'Have you considered how others might view this situation? Could other factors be at play?' Encourage them to consider alternative perspectives.
  - 'We all have our own biases and perspectives. It's important to be open to the possibility that we might not have all the answers.' Highlight the potential for bias and blind spots.

- *Focus on facts and logic:*
  - 'Research shows that *[alternative solution]* can be effective in achieving similar goals.' Present evidence that supports alternative approaches.
  - 'By refusing to compromise, we risk alienating others and creating unnecessary conflict.' Highlight the potential risks and downsides of their rigid stance.

Power Game: Sniping

Sniping behaviour often masks the true nature of the Fanatic's feelings, as they use universal, global statements to hide their own concerns. They may use phrases like:

- 'Everyone says …'
- 'Lots of people think …'
- 'Others are concerned that …'

Cause: Reduced confidence in their perspective

If the Fanatic is not confident in their complaint, or is concerned about how they will be perceived if they express it fully, they may use a blanket statement.

Counter moves

- *Create clear channels for feedback and constructive conflict to help eliminate the vague aspersions that are really covert power moves:* Failing that, double down on specifics and accountability. Ask them for examples, in writing, sent to the appropriate channel.

- *Try these helpful phrases as needed:*
    - 'That's an interesting observation. Can you give me a few examples of individuals and what they said and when?'
    - 'Those are indeed concerning allegations. It would be great if you could gather statements from those concerned so we can address the issues directly in a transparent and open way.'
    - 'Thank you for raising these issues. Sounds like we need a full appraisal of the situation. Can you and the people who have these concerns draft some suggestions for improvements?'

* * *

The shift from Guardian to its shadow archetype of the Fanatic often stems from fear, attachment or a desire for control. As the Fanatic, the individual clings to the past, becomes defensive and resists change by playing Power Games such as gatekeeping, obstructing and undermining progress. By becoming too fixated on their perspective, they lose influence and hinder the forward movement of the organisation. Understanding these causes allows you to create strategies to help the Guardian stay balanced, focused on protecting the best while embracing healthy progress.

To keep the Guardian from becoming the Fanatic, focus on maintaining flexibility, encouraging open dialogue and honouring the past while embracing progress. Through balanced frameworks for risk management, sharing decision-making authority and fostering trust in new leadership, the Guardian can protect what's best in the organisation without slipping into rigidity or obstructionism.

By developing the practice of questioning your thinking and surfacing assumptions within your team and organisation, you can disable the tendency to Fanaticism. In the meantime, encouraging your fanatic colleague to dial back the rhetoric can be an exercise in patience. Bite your tongue, encourage gently.

NO GUTS, NO GLORY

Lincoln stood beside his lead engineer in front of the giant display screen. He squinted at the blueprints his colleague was explaining.

'What I'm saying, Lincoln, is that asteroid mining is still untested. We know some elements, but what we don't know for sure is how far the debris field will extend when we use explosives to get at the minerals we need. Drilling might be the safest option.'

'But more expensive and slow,' replied Lincoln as he folded his arms. 'What are the risks with our next project?'

'The asteroid we are looking at is close to Moon operations. The Gateway Moon orbit station and Artemis could potentially come into the fallout field if we time it wrong.'

'How likely is that?'

"The window to get it right is small. If we get it wrong, there's a 50 per cent chance the fallout will hit the Moon. It might miss the human infrastructure.'

'And if we get the right timing, no chance of impact?' The engineer nodded. Lincoln tapped his chin. 'I'll take those odds. Explosives it is. Have drilling ready as well, but my preference is for explosives. And good timing.' Lincoln grinned and punched his engineer lightly on the shoulder.

CHAPTER 12

THE PIONEER AND THE GAMBLER

When we are brimming with progressive ideas and alive with creativity, we're embodying the Pioneer archetype. We feel bold and brash and want to bolt ahead with new projects. Our Conch can become worn out from the advocacy we are doing for these exciting new paths. If we lose sight of our collective accountability, however, we can grow into the shadow archetype of the Pioneer – the Gambler.

Reining in a Gambler

Dealing with a Gambler is much like trying to tame a wild horse. Their energy is unbounded and they just want to run free, regardless of who they trample. Time to get your lasso and rein in that beast.

Power Game: Cutting corners

Gamblers bypass established processes and approval systems, rushing decisions without considering potential pitfalls. They may push projects through by cutting corners or manipulating timelines to get results faster, disregarding the checks and balances meant to ensure long-term success.

Cause: Impatience with process

The Gambler, eager to implement new ideas, might become frustrated with the slow pace of progress or the need for thorough vetting. This impatience can lead to risky decisions, bypassing due diligence.

Counter moves

- *Highlight the risks and potential consequences:*
  - 'I understand you're trying to get things done quickly. First to market is an important consideration. At the same time, I'm concerned that cutting corners on *[specific process]* could lead to *[potential problems]*.' Express your concerns constructively.
  - 'Remember what happened last time we skipped *[process]*? It ended up costing us *[time/money/resources]* to fix it.' Provide examples of past issues or near misses.
  - 'While it might seem faster now, cutting corners could create bigger problems down the line and jeopardise the success of the project.' Focus on the bigger picture and long-term impact.

- *Emphasise the importance of established processes:*
  - 'Even though we may not like it, these processes are in place for a reason. They help us ensure quality, consistency and compliance.' Explain the rationale behind the processes.
  - 'By following the established procedures, we can minimise errors, reduce risks and ensure that we're meeting all the necessary requirements.' Highlight the potential benefits of following procedures.
  - 'If you're finding the processes cumbersome or confusing, I'm happy to help you navigate them or find ways to streamline them.' Offer support and assistance in navigating the processes.

- *Appeal to their sense of responsibility and professionalism:*
  - 'We all have a responsibility to uphold the standards and integrity of our work.' Remind them of their obligations.
  - 'I know you take pride in your work. Let's make sure we're delivering high-quality results.' Appeal to their professional pride.

Power Game: The lone wolf

The Gambler can isolate themselves, believing their ideas are too bold for others to understand. They make unilateral decisions and may even reject collaboration, seeing it as slowing down their creative momentum. This approach risks alienating others and leading to poorly vetted projects.

Cause: Overconfidence in personal vision

The Gambler may become overly confident in their ideas, believing they alone have the vision to see the future clearly. This overconfidence can lead to reckless decisions, as they start to gamble on their own insight rather than seeking input from others.

Counter moves:

- *Appreciate their strengths (and gently highlight the gaps):*
  - 'I really admire your innovative thinking and your ability to come up with bold ideas.' Acknowledge their unique perspective and creativity.
  - 'I'd love to hear more about your vision for this project. Can you share some of your thoughts with me?' Express your interest in their ideas.
  - 'Sometimes, bouncing ideas off others can lead to even better solutions and help us avoid potential pitfalls.' Gently point out the benefits of collaboration.

- *Build bridges and foster connection:*
    - 'Hey, I was just grabbing a coffee. Want to join me?' Create opportunities for informal interaction by inviting them to lunch, coffee or a casual brainstorming session.
    - 'That's a really interesting approach. Can you tell me more about how you came up with that idea?' Show genuine interest in their work by asking questions, offering feedback and expressing your appreciation for their efforts.
    - 'I noticed you're also interested in *[topic]*. Have you seen *[article/book/event]*?' Find common ground and shared interests. Look for areas where you can connect on a personal or professional level.

- *Encourage collaboration without demanding it:*
    - 'I think your idea has great potential. Perhaps we could involve a few others to get their feedback and refine it further.' Frame collaboration as a way to enhance their ideas.
    - 'How about we have a quick brainstorming session with a couple of colleagues to explore different perspectives?' Suggest small-scale collaborative efforts.
    - 'By involving others, we can tap into a wider range of knowledge and experience, which can lead to more robust solutions.' Highlight the benefits of diverse perspectives.

Power Game: Going rogue

Gamblers embrace a rogue mentality, acting independently of the group's consensus or established protocols. They may present their initiatives as 'now or never' opportunities, pressuring others to get on board quickly without fully exploring alternatives or considering potential risks.

Cause: Fatigue from advocacy

Constantly advocating for new ideas and fighting resistance can wear the Pioneer/Gambler down, leading them to take drastic steps to push through their agenda. This fatigue can cause them to gamble on bold moves just to overcome inertia.

Counter moves

- *Appeal to the collective good:*
  - 'I understand you're excited about this opportunity, so it's important that we work together as a team and make decisions that benefit everyone, not just individual projects.' Emphasise the importance of teamwork and shared goals.
  - 'By involving others in the decision-making process, we can ensure that we're considering all angles and making informed choices.' Highlight the value of diverse perspectives and collaboration.
  - 'Going rogue can create confusion and disrupt the workflow for other team members. It's important to consider the impact of our actions on the whole group.' Remind them of the potential impact on others.

- *Encourage transparency and communication:*
  - 'I appreciate your initiative. It's also important to keep everyone informed about your plans and progress. Can we find a way to share information more effectively?' Express your desire to be kept in the loop.
  - 'Perhaps we could have a quick weekly meeting to discuss ongoing projects and ensure that everyone is on the same page.' Suggest regular check-ins or progress updates.
  - 'If you're feeling pressured or have concerns, it's important to communicate them openly so we can find solutions together.' Encourage open and honest communication.

- *Highlight the risks and benefits of collaboration:*
  - 'I appreciate your willingness to take initiative and explore new ideas. However, it's important to balance that with a collaborative approach.' Acknowledge the potential benefits of their independent approach.

- 'Acting independently can lead to duplicated efforts, missed opportunities and increased risks. By working together, we can mitigate those risks and achieve better results.' Point out the potential risks of going rogue.

- 'If you're feeling overwhelmed or need help with certain aspects of the project, don't hesitate to reach out to the team. We're here to support you.' Offer support and assistance.

- *Set boundaries and expectations:*
    - 'I understand that you're eager to move forward. It's also important to follow the established procedures and get the necessary approvals before proceeding.' Gently but firmly remind them of established protocols.
    - 'I'm a bit concerned that we didn't have a chance to fully discuss this initiative before it was launched. Can we make sure we have more collaborative discussions in the future?' Express your concerns about the lack of consultation.
    - 'While individual initiative is valuable, it's also important to respect the decisions made by the team as a whole.' Reinforce the importance of respecting team decisions.

Power Game: Renegading

Gamblers push ahead with projects despite concerns or objections from others, positioning themselves as a visionary misunderstood by more cautious colleagues. They may ignore red flags or bypass consensus-building processes, framing their actions as bold leadership when they're actually disregarding collective accountability.

Cause: Resistance to feedback

If the Gambler becomes resistant to feedback or scepticism from others, they may start to gamble on ideas out of frustration. They might see feedback as stifling their creativity rather than as a necessary part of refining and testing ideas.

Counter moves

- *Appeal to shared responsibility and accountability:*
  - 'I understand your passion for this project. It's also important to remember that we're all in this together. We share responsibility for its success or failure.' Highlight the importance of collective ownership.
  - 'By involving others in the process, we can ensure that we're considering all perspectives and making informed choices that benefit the whole team.' Emphasise the value of collaborative decision-making.
  - 'Ignoring concerns and bypassing consensus can lead to resentment, conflict and, ultimately, jeopardise the success of the project.' Remind the Gambler of the potential consequences of going it alone.

- *Encourage open communication and feedback:*
  - 'I appreciate your enthusiasm. I'm also a bit concerned about *[specific concern]*. Can we discuss this openly and find a way to address it?' Create a safe space for expressing concerns.
  - 'I understand you see this as a bold move. Can you help me understand why you feel it's necessary to bypass the usual process?' Actively listen to their perspective.
  - 'I think your idea has merit. Perhaps we could also explore *[alternative approach]*, which might address some of the concerns raised by the team.' Offer constructive feedback and alternative suggestions.

- *Highlight the value of consensus and collaboration:*
  - 'When we work together and make decisions collaboratively, we create a stronger sense of ownership and commitment to the project's success.' Emphasise the benefits of a united team.

- 'Remember that project where we all worked together and achieved amazing results? We can do that again if we harness the collective wisdom of the team.' Showcase examples of successful collaborative projects.

- 'We all have a role to play in ensuring the success of our projects. By working together and respecting each other's contributions, we can achieve great things.' Promote a culture of shared responsibility.

***

The shift from Pioneer to Gambler is often caused by impatience, overconfidence, fatigue or pressure to deliver quick results. As the Gambler, the individual plays risky Power Games such as cutting corners, making unilateral decisions and bypassing accountability, driven by the desire to push ahead without fully considering the consequences. To maintain the integrity of the Pioneer, it's essential they stay grounded in collective accountability, remain open to feedback, and ensure that bold moves are tempered with careful planning and collaboration.

Much of the excesses of the Gambler, and indeed the other shadow archetypes, can be constrained by having good team processes in place. In the next part, I explore what you can do to build team and organisational structures that minimise Power Games.

PART IV

BUILDING HEALTHY POWER STRUCTURES

Here's what I know: cultures in teams and organisations go through cycles, much like the seasons in a garden. The fallow soil of a new team or organisation is full of potential and promise. Seeds are planted, and the team sends out shoots and begins to flourish. Soon enough, the team is 'ripe', with ideas and projects ready for harvest, after much labour and effort. This level of production, of course, is not always sustainable, and a period of rest, or laying fallow, is required before a new season begins.

If leaders do not tend their 'garden' – that is, their team or organisation – in each of these phases, all hell can break loose. Weeds overrun the shoots of new effort, the garden falls into disarray and disrepair, and instead of laying fallow during rest, the garden rots and goes putrid.

The good news is that we can begin again at any phase and reinvigorate the culture – the following chapters show you how.

A TEAM OF STARS OR A STAR TEAM?

'How is it going to work, Maja?' Xanthe stared at the holo display as Maja went through the logistics for the Olympus Project selection process. Xanthe had just agreed to take on the role as lead designer for the tender bid, working alongside superstars Troy Bruin and Xavier Consus. Two men used to being in charge.

'You'll have final say on the overall design. I expect you to defer to the expertise of Troy when it comes to psychological health in human habitat design, and on Xavier for food cultivation.'

'Will they listen to me? I've been out of the Gaia world for a while now.' Xanthe rubbed her neck and grimaced. She anticipated a lot of one-upmanship with those egos.

'Oh, Xanthe, you know what to do. Start with the basics. Set up your team structure. It's the best antidote to any dramas. Good culture needs good seeds. Start there.'

CHAPTER 13

HEALTHY POWER STRUCTURES IN TEAMS

Every leader I've worked with seeks a great team culture. After all, working with high performers in a fun, friendly environment with a strong sense of camaraderie and common purpose is enlivening. And, let's face it, the opposite sucks. Showing up to work with disenchanted, gossipy, undermining, miserable colleagues is soul-destroying.

I've seen it happen many times: well-intentioned, enthusiastic leaders bring their team together, and things go well for a while. Until they don't. The 'garden' I just talked about is overrun with weeds, and good ideas and projects start to rot.

So, how do we begin? How do we tend our culture garden?

First – and to add another layer to our metaphor – we need a bicycle.

A bicycle gives you the energy and mobility to ride around the various pockets of your garden, tending to weed infestations, watering and feeding your plants, and generally encouraging a positive growing environment.

How are you doing? That's two metaphors we're working with now: the garden is our workplace culture, vast with hidden pockets, while the bicycle is our team, powerful and capable when built right.

Got it? Good. Let's carry on.

The high-performing team bicycle

A well-built, high-performing team bicycle creates healthy power structures in teams, as shown in the following figure.

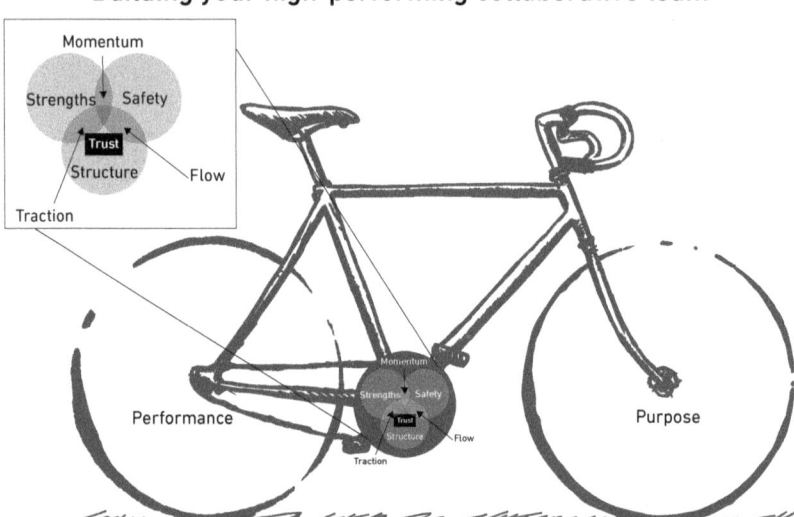

Building your high-performing collaborative team

Purpose

The front wheel in your high-performing team bicycle is your *purpose*. As a team, you need to know why you exist, and how you fit into the bigger picture. How does your team bicycle serve the greater culture garden? Do you work in one area or do you ride through all sections?

Once you know your team's purpose, you need to articulate this purpose in a simple statement. For example:

> *We are the social media marketing team. We provide stories online so that our customers, stakeholders and community know about the work we do and how they can interact with us.*

Just keep your purpose statement simple: 'We do x so that y.'

Performance

If purpose is your front wheel, then the back wheel is your *performance*. The back wheel naturally follows the front wheel (duh) while also driving your forward momentum. Interestingly, though, many teams fail to identify clearly what outcomes they are trying to achieve.

For greater clarity on outcomes, I always refer to my good friend Stacey Barr's work on key performance indicators. Her methodology is simple: start with results. What do you want to see, hear, touch, taste, feel and experience at the end of your activity? These are your results. Define the outcomes that demonstrate progress towards a fulfilment of this vision and strategic goals. After that, you can develop measures that track the impact of the work and progress towards the vision.

You need to include measures for ethical leadership and a healthy, equitable, inclusive culture. However, it's also essential you measure individual and collective contributions. No one person is responsible for the collective outcomes.

Going back to our social media marketing team example, their intended results might include the following:

- People know about our work.
- People tell others about our work.
- Customers refer us to others.
- People share our stories with others.
- People ask us about our work.

Notice how these example results don't include 'engagement'. While the listed outcomes may indicate engagement, they do so by describing specific behaviours. When you get specific about the behaviours and outcomes, you avoid what Stacey calls 'weasel words' – words that sound important but are fluffy and hard to pin down.

You want to nail your results with tangible specifics. This is essential for accountability. Once you've determined your required results and outcomes, you can then build measures to track your effectiveness.

Adding on gears: Structure

Every bicycle has a set of gears. This is the magic of bike technology: gears leverage your effort. When it comes to your team bicycle, the primary gear is structure. This is how you organise your work and agree on how to work together. This is also how you build in brakes and safeguards against power abuse.

There's a lot to take in here, so grab a cup of tea and a notebook, and prepare to make notes.

Governance: Building triangles

Governance is a set of agreements that lays out the important components for how you will run operations. Its primary purpose is to make interactions transparent and accountable. (Unless you're a psychopath, in which case the role of governance is to obscure and hide your manipulations. But that's not you, so let's continue.)

When thinking about governance, using a triangle structure is useful. At the top of the triangle is someone who has the authority to make the final call. They might also have accountability for those decisions, owning up when things go wrong. Authority, accountability and responsibility are a hierarchy of power and activity, and should be clearly defined. To ensure that the person at the top of the triangle doesn't go bonkers and become drunk on power, you also need a Code of Ethics to outline your rules of the game.

Transparent reporting lines and job descriptions are used to define roles, responsibilities and who is accountable for what decisions. Note that accountability often sits alongside authority.

Authority

Authority is who gets to have the final say. Authority might be relegated solely to one position; however, this is usually a bad idea because it sets up an easy pathway for Tyrants (refer to chapter 8). More sensibly, authority is distributed to different roles within a framework.

For example, the designated team facilitator might have the authority of the final vote to break an impasse on a team. The head of social media marketing might have the authority for budget spend up to a certain amount.

Accountability

Accountability indicates who takes full ownership of the performance of the task, system or unit. This is largely in relation to when things go belly up, and your team needs someone to apologise and sort out the mess. This creates an impetus to make sure things do not go off track, because no-one likes to own up to a mess. It can also result in arse-covering exercises and imperious constraints. If the rest of your processes are poor, these types of Power Games can easily sneak in. For more on this, see the section 'Process: Adding in circles', later in this chapter.

Responsibility

By setting responsibility, you nominate who is actually doing the work. This may be the same person who has accountability, but not always. For example, the head of social media marketing may have accountability for the unit's performance, but may not themselves be responsible for posting or managing various campaigns.

Code of Ethics

Most leaders think they are 'ethical'. They believe they are essentially good and will make the right choices when confronted with dilemmas. These good intentions can go awry, however, when leaders are under pressure in a crisis. In such circumstances, a Code of Ethics can help with trickier decisions. Your Code may include aspects such as your commitment to integrity, honesty, transparency, respect and care for the environment, and use of a supply chain free from human rights abuses. It should also clearly define acceptable behaviour, especially regarding power dynamics.

See appendix A for a sample Code of Ethics, and see the resources available via the Power Games website https://www.zoerouth.com/power-games-bonus-material for more on ethical decision making.

Your team's (and organisation's) leaders should be trained in ethical leadership models, where the focus is on growing and serving others, rather than on accruing power.

The triangles model outlines this hierarchy of power and Crown-wearing; however, it's your process that keeps things in check.

Process: Adding in circles

Considering your processes is when it's useful to think in circles. Your power lines might form triangles, but to prevent runaway Power Games, you need to operate in circles as much as possible. This means being consultative and collaborative, egalitarian and inclusive in your processes.

Decisions

Transparent decision-making is at the heart of sensible power management. First, you need to identify what kinds of decisions your team can make – for example, do these decisions relate to recruitment? Spending? Projects? Experiments? Equally important is identifying decisions you and your team cannot make, such as starting a new product line or changing your organisation's mission.

Then you need to determine how decisions are made – for example, via democratic voting? Consultative? Autocratic? Holacratic? (See appendix D for more on holacratic decision-making.) How do you then record your decisions? When will you review your decisions to check the success of your assumptions and frameworks?

When making these decisions, keep in mind that in methods such as consensus-based decision-making or participatory budgeting, employees at different levels have a voice in resource allocation and significant decisions. This, in turn, helps share power and reduce Power Games.

Delegation

Sometimes we need to share work. The gaslighter Manipulator can take advantage of this and deflect work on to others. With clear delegation rules, however, you can stamp out this tendency. To form a good delegation, ask:

- What work can we delegate to others?
- Is this delegation within the team or outside of the team? Within the organisation or outside of it?
- What are other boundaries or limits to delegation?

Deadlines

Deadlines are often a touchy area, especially with plenty of interdependencies in team work. Therefore, it's essential to have a clear, common understanding of the respective, interlocking deadlines. Here are some questions to consider:

- How do we determine deadlines?
- How do we manage deadline dependencies?
- How do we make these transparent to all?
- How do we update deadlines and project progress in real time, especially with co-dependent deadlines?

Ethical framework

Aside from the Code of Ethics, an ethical framework helps to determine the filters you will use for decision-making. A useful way to create this framework is to list the team's values and ethical standards, and then prioritise them.

For example, if you had to choose between missing a deadline and possibly the contract and staff safety, which will you choose? Or, if the sustainable choice will cost the customer 50 per cent more, what do you choose? Pre-empting the 'rock and a hard place' choices by pitting your values against one another helps create an ethical decision-making framework for the team and its members.

Conflict resolution

Occasionally, conflict may emerge. This can range from misunderstandings to disagreements about the team's approach to genuine rancour about another person's behaviour. What is the process that the team agrees is the best way to resolve conflict and disputes? And what will you do if the conflict is with the team leader?

Sometimes teams come up with code words to indicate disgruntlement during a meeting. Brené Brown wrote that her team uses the phrase, 'the story I am telling myself right now is …' as a cue to share difficult emotions that arise when in discussion with others. She has also shared the team uses the phrase, 'I need to rumble with you …' as code for, 'I need to roll this weird feeling around with you to see if we can come to a common understanding of what is going on'.

I had another team use the word 'pineapple' to cut through talking over one another. It was a good circuit breaker – we don't often use the word 'pineapple' and so it was easy to capture everyone's attention.

Having some basic agreements about how you might resolve conflict is also helpful. For example, you may include something like, 'No triangles' (hat tip to Rachael Robertson and her work). This means that you will not discuss the problem with a third person and engage in toxic gossip; instead, you will deal with the other person directly.

Improving communication

Ah, yes. Communication. Every single team with whom I run culture workshops declares they want 'better communication'.

Everyone nods their head solemnly in agreement, revealing the common angst over communication gone wrong.

However, when I ask them to say exactly what they mean by 'better communication', it takes a few minutes to get specific. Here are some prompts to help you and your team get crystal clear on what 'better communication' means for you.

Meetings

Why should you meet? When should you meet? For how long? About what? What is the agenda? Who will prepare the agenda and facilitate the meeting? What kind of meeting is it (decision-making, problem-solving, strategic thinking, debriefing, celebration)? Knowing the answers to these kinds of questions helps you plan your meeting schedule and type of meeting, and run them efficiently.

Reporting

Who reports to whom, by when, on what and how frequently? Who else needs to know about x, y and z? How and when will you update them? Which communication platform or tool will you and your team use for what? (This could include email, text, WhatsApp, intranet, video message and written briefs.)

Also keep in mind that reporting doesn't just flow upwards. Regularly gather and analyse feedback from all levels of the organisation (peers, subordinates, supervisors) to assess leadership performance. This ensures that leaders are held accountable by multiple stakeholders, not just their superiors. Also include independent audits of decision-making processes, and track financial transactions to help prevent unchecked power. Also consider asking external consultants to provide an impartial review.

Debriefing

What do you need to debrief? This could include debriefing at the end of an experiment, following a safety incident or accident, or even on your meeting process. Also consider who can call a debrief. How often will you do this? Where? When? Who will chair this meeting?

Feedback

How will you seek, give and receive feedback? On what topics? Do you have a common way of doing this? Do you have individual preferences about how you like to receive feedback? How do you get feedback about your team's performance? How frequently should you seek this out? How will you do this? Whom will you ask?

Share the team's updates, key decisions, challenges and triumphs on as many communication platforms as possible to minimise assumptions and gossip. Create 'listening circles' where managers can listen to the challenges and concerns of employees, and then commit to addressing these to close the feedback loop.

Behaviours: Developing your Culture Compass

Team behaviour is where Power Games can take hold if you do not detail the kinds of behaviours you accept and support, and those you do not. Surprisingly, people often think this is just common sense – after all, doesn't everyone know what behaving 'professional' actually means? It turns out, no. Not everyone has the same idea about professionalism. Or respect. Or kindness.

In one team, the team members shared that 'professional' meant not sharing weekend drunken escapades on a Monday with colleagues. For some, hearing about such escapades diminished their colleague in their eyes. They also did not want to hear about them because they felt it normalised excessive alcohol consumption, something they were actively against. In another team, one person shared they felt hearing about their colleague's sex life was unprofessional and unwanted.

Some were shocked to hear about these objections, never thinking their friendly sharing was anything other than rapport-building. Here's the thing about humans, however: we are all different and have different lenses on the world.

Some people think swearing in the workplace is normal and authentic. Others think it is the height of rudeness. We won't know about these different values and objections until we talk about them.

I encourage teams to develop their own Culture Compass, as I describe it in my book *Loyalty* (2018). This captures critical agreements in the following compass points:

- *North point:* What we care about, our values.
- *East point:* Our purpose – who we serve or help.
- *West point:* Our results.
- *South point:* Agreed behaviours, standards and norms.

Charter and Code of Conduct

The South point of this Culture Compass, agreed behaviours, is the one area people find awkward to discuss. Consider the 'sex life' conversation. The offended person feels awkward raising it because they don't want their colleague to feel weird or embarrassed. So they continue feeling awkward themselves as their colleague expounds the virtues of role plays and toys.

Some of this work is about expressing boundaries and what is okay and not okay for each individual. Some of this work is about surfacing what is commonly acceptable, or not, for the group. I encourage teams to write a list of things they *don't* want in their team behaviours, being very specific, and then write what they *do* want, again with specific examples. Another way of looking at this is considering 'above the line' behaviours (ownership, accountability, responsibility) and 'below the line' behaviours (blame, excuses, denial). This is the OAR and BED model, developed by Roger Connors, Tom Smith and Craig R Hickman in their work on accountability and leadership, and outlined in their book *The Oz Principle: Getting Results Through Individual and Organizational Accountability*.

I ask teams to be specific to avoid any continued misunderstandings. Saying you don't want 'disrespect' and you do want 'respect', for example, is not helpful, because respect, like professionalism, has many interpretations. For some, respect means showing up on time or early. For others, respect means giving the benefit of the doubt when someone is late (because it could have been due to traffic, a chronically ill child, or even one's own personal ailment).

If you don't say what bothers you, your colleagues won't know. So get it out in the open.

Once your team has determined, in specific terms, what they do and don't want in terms of behaviour, you can create a Code of Conduct. This is a more formal document where you can cover aspects such as maintaining confidentiality of your customers, not speaking ill of the employer when out in public, and being a good ambassador for the organisation when wearing the team's logo. I've provided a sample Code of Conduct in appendix B.

Collaboration Handbook

Some of the most revealing conversations when I facilitate with teams occur when I ask them to share their personal preferences in how they like to work. Using a set list of questions, I ask them about things like pet peeves, sharing strengths, known 'blind spots' and how they like to receive feedback. I find this exercise is a quick way for everyone to get familiar with the working modes of their colleagues, and to work better with them. I set up a shareable Google sheet so the entire team can see each other's responses. (See appendix C for the full list of questions.)

You can then combine these responses to create your team's Collaboration Handbook. These responses, captured in a central location, become a shortcut for 'getting to know you' with colleagues. You could also include your Culture Charter and your larger Culture Compass with the Handbook, and then use the Handbook as part of employee or team induction.

Imagine starting at a workplace and your colleagues being able to walk you through 'how we do things around here' in explicit terms, with all these fabulous details all laid out. No more guessing who does what and how they like to be approached, or finding out the hard way that Cyril prefers meetings in the afternoon and definitely not to be interrupted between 9 am and 10 am when he is online in meetings with overseas clients. Perhaps you also discover that Harriet enjoys crochet and does parkrun every Saturday, just like you. Now you have something in common and a way to build some collegiate social bridges. Yeeha!

Inclusion and belonging

One of the joys of working in teams is to feel part of something, and to feel like we belong. This notion of belonging brings with it a primal sense of safety. We are tribal creatures, and we are safer when part of a tribe: the group will protect us, make us feel welcome, wanted and valued.

But building this sense of belonging does not happen on its own. We need to be intentional about this through our recruitment, onboarding and off-boarding processes. Also important are the acknowledgement and celebration of achievements.

Recruitment practices

Implement comprehensive diversity, equity and inclusion (DEI) policies to ensure diversity in hiring and track the progress of underrepresented groups in leadership roles.

Onboarding

Onboarding new employees is an obvious time to make an impression and welcome someone into the team, while also outlining expectations, norms, structure and processes. A way to build trust quickly is to hold a meeting where everyone shares their role and experience, including the newcomer, so people can get a sense of what the new person is capable of before they get going. Making a big deal of new arrivals is a lovely way to help people feel welcome and wanted.

Off-boarding

How you send people on their way also matters. It signals what kind of team you have, and how you treat others. If you've done a good job with your team processes, then this need not be an awkward, horrible moment. It could be a celebration of that person's contribution.

Now, if someone breaches the Code of Conduct or fails to adhere to the Culture Compass, then it's a different story. Send this toxic performer on their way sooner rather than later. Debrief with the team afterwards to take any lessons from the experience.

Acknowledgment

In *Drive: The Surprising Truth About What Motivates Us*, Dan Pink noted that one of the things that creates a great place to work is acknowledgment – that is, recognition for one's effort and contributions. Acknowledging team mates' successes and achievements is such a simple, no-cost way of building engagement. And yet we can get so caught up in meeting deadlines and busy-ness we lose the opportunity to make people feel valued. Simple acknowledgment and recognition go a long way.

Celebrations

Celebrating progress and achievements individually and collectively is a great people-oriented way of building rapport and bonds between team members. Emphasising the collective success can also unwind any propensity to Power Games. When the collective is emphasised, there is less room for jostling.

Reward

Conversely, offering rewards is where things can get tricky. How do we recognise individual effort and collective success via rewards? It's a tension to manage. While we may be working collaboratively to achieve outcomes, individuals also contribute and work hard in their own right. We don't want to obfuscate one for the other. If we get the balance wrong, Power Games can run wild with jealousy and create much subterfuge.

The best kinds of rewards are those predicated on demonstration of the organisation's or team's values. You might combine these rewards in a celebration or acknowledgment ceremony where employees are singled out for demonstrating the best of the culture's values and norms.

What gets rewarded gets repeated. Choose wisely.

Values-based recognition and promotions

Integrate the organisation's values into performance review and promotion processes. Leaders should be chosen not just for their skills and results, but also for their commitment to the organisation's values and ethical standards.

***

That was a very long exploration of team structure – the first and most important gear in the high-performing team bicycle. There's a lot to it! Once we have this gear nailed down and working well, though, the rest is a bit easier.

Adding a second gear: Strengths

The further research Dan Pink shares in *Drive* also shows that when people grow and develop their existing strengths and skills, they are more likely to be engaged. Use any sort of profiling instrument to surface these natural inclinations. I like to use DiSC (standing for the four behaviour styles of dominance, influence, steadiness and conscientiousness); however, you could use another analysis tool, such as Herrmann-Brain Dominance Instrument (HBDI, which measures four integrated systems of thinking preferences). The idea here is to lean into each person's strengths and natural tendencies and develop those strengths as superpowers, while also being mindful of the blind spots of these strengths under pressure.

Developing people's strengths is also about supporting their skill development and technical expertise. This is an essential stage in the development of leadership maturity; when we develop a deeper grounding in our primary profession, we gain a solid sense of esteem. Our Cauldron boils a little hotter, we throw a few coins in our Coin bag, and we start experimenting with our Conch as we speak up.

Diversity

One of the best ways to strengthen the entire team is to ensure diversity – including diverse perspectives, experiences, thought processes and cognition. Having a mix of backgrounds, experiences and perspectives can help to challenge groupthink and prevent a homogeneous culture from taking root.

Succession planning

Succession planning is very easily said, and so rarely done well. Develop and communicate a clear succession plan for leadership roles to avoid long-term stagnation in power. Regularly rotate leaders and high-level managers to introduce fresh perspectives. Acting roles are a huge opportunity for individuals to gain experience in leadership and for the team to inoculate against leader-dependency.

Leadership development programs

Of course, I am going to advocate for leadership development. I've been a leadership consultant, trainer and facilitator for almost 40 years at the time of writing. I believe in the power of giving individuals the experience of leading in a controlled environment as an adjunct to their workplace experiences. Invest in leadership development programs to nurture internal talent and prepare future leaders, helping to create a pipeline of capable leaders who can step into roles when needed.

Training ethics and power

Offer regular training on ethical leadership, bias awareness and power dynamics to keep leaders (and future leaders) mindful of how their behaviour impacts others.

Culture of learning

Learning is more than just attending leadership programs. It's about our mindset and how we tackle our experiences every day.

Promote a team culture where failures and mistakes are openly discussed and seen as opportunities for growth. This can help prevent a culture of secrecy where leaders hide failures to protect their power. If you have your debriefs and experiment reviews set up as part of your structure gear, you're already halfway there. You also need to be positive during these processes to set the tone. If you're the team leader, set the example by exploring failure and lessons learned first.

Advocacy

Advocacy, through an employee advocacy group, can be a formal way to encourage the use of collective Conch. Create formal mechanisms for employees to come together to advocate for their interests, such as through employee councils or task forces. These groups can serve as a counterbalance to unchecked leadership authority.

Autonomy

Looking again at some of the lessons from *Drive*, Dan Pink tells us that autonomy is one of the key drivers of engagement. People love making their own decisions. Give team members the ability to operate with more autonomy, making decisions within their scope without having to rely on top–down directives for everything. This decentralisation reduces the likelihood of power being hoarded at the top.

Working the third gear: Safety

Psychological safety is where people feel safe to share ideas without the fear of ridicule – in other words, toxic Power Games are absent. Everything we've done to this point is hoping to establish psychological safety for the team. Extra attention can be put on this element to ensure safety is well cared for.

Forums

Regular, structured forums for open dialogue, such as town hall meetings or open-door policies, can assist with keeping the conversation about safety open.

Set up regular check-ins where employees are invited to provide honest feedback on leadership, culture and their experience in the organisation. Ensure avenues exist for this feedback to reach leadership and be acted on, with responses then reported back to the entire staff.

Experiments

Run experiments as part of the strategic business process. Model designing a hypothesis, challenging assumptions, being prepared to be wrong, collecting data and analysing the results, including 'failures'. Model 'lessons learned' in these experiments as a way of normalising feedback as a healthy part of organisational and individual growth.

Coaching culture

Practise giving and receiving feedback one on one and in teams to normalise the experience of growth conversations.

Rotation and limits on tenure

Set term limits for senior leadership positions to prevent the stagnation of ideas and power. Even if a leader stays in the organisation, rotating them to a different role or responsibility can help prevent power abuse.

Also conduct regular leadership reviews, where the performance, values alignment and behaviour of top executives are assessed by both internal stakeholders (such as the board) and external consultants.

As the bicycle moves: The gears in action

This is the exciting part. You have your front wheel pointed where you want to go. You know your back wheel will follow along and drive the outcomes you said were important. Let's now look at what happens once you activate the gears.

Structure and strengths: Traction

When you and your team know how you fit, how decisions are made, how reporting lines and accountabilities are set out, and that you all are developing your skills, then you gain *traction*. You and your team move with focus and clarity against your individual and team goals with less friction.

Strengths and safety: Momentum

As your expertise develops and you feel safe to fail and experiment, you and the team take more measured risks, and the *momentum* builds in the team's activities.

Safety and structure: Flow

When you and your team feel comfortable sharing ideas, exploring new concepts and experiments, all within the practical confines and clear processes encased in your team structures, you can experience *flow*: deep focus and productivity.

All working together: Trust

Much has been made of trust in teams. In my opinion, starting with trust as the first topic in the conversation about team high performance is a mistake.

Trust is a by-product of the high-performing team bicycle. When you and your team have a clear purpose, you know your intended results and track your progress towards them in a well-structured team that leverages strengths and builds safety mechanisms, then you experience trust between team members.

If there's no trust, chances are one of the other components of the bicycle is missing. This is good news because you know where to start. You don't need to go about moaning about the lack of trust between team members – you take action to create the conditions where trust can develop.

Distributing power in collaborative groups

Collaborative groups form when individuals come together for a common goal, while still representing different teams, organisations, interests or stakeholders. Some examples of collaborative groups are:

- cross-functional project teams
- industry associations
- membership groups
- cooperative research centres
- cooperatives
- boards
- local councils.

These groups are especially ripe for Power Games because group members often come with Crowns from their own area of expertise, operate independently, or have strong vested interests.

In the case of local councils, divergent values and belief systems can also add to the tumultuous process of trying to find common ground without resorting to Power Games.

The same principles and processes apply as outlined so far in this book:

- Individually, develop the Four Spheres of Power.
- Set up your high-performing team bicycle.
- Ensure your organisational power systems are constrained with good policies and practices.

Group monitoring

In the following sections, I outline some additional practices and processes that may assist collaborative, leader-less, flat hierarchy groups.

Five aspects need to be monitored, and anyone in the group may elect or be nominated to take on one of these roles.

Deliverables

In this role, the individual holds the whole group to account and asks gritty, tangible questions, such as:

- Do we have the resources to accomplish this goal?
- Who will actually do the work?
- Are we meeting our deadlines?
- Is the quality up to scratch?
- Who is and isn't keeping their commitments?
- What's sliding through the cracks?

Big picture

This role monitors the group's overall efforts and focus. The individual can ask questions such as:

- Are we living and working by our values?
- Are we making progress towards our vision?
- What's on the horizon that may assist or hinder us?
- What are the internal and external factors that may get in our way?

Process

Not for the faint-hearted, this role tackles process and how the group is treating its obligations and each other. The individual might check and highlight things such as the following:

- increased emotional temperature on issues and discussions
- surreptitious Power Games such as gossip, back-channelling and undermining
- groupthink and echo chambers that keep new ideas at bay
- inappropriate behaviour
- breaches of the Code of Conduct and Code of Ethics.

Communication

The role acts as a connector. The individual asks questions like, 'Who needs to know about this?', 'Who needs to be consulted?' and 'Who will be affected by this?' By ensuring the messages are clear and distributed effectively across the right channels, the communication role minimises gossip, innuendo and assumptions between team members, and with stakeholders and those outside the organisation.

Energy

This is the cultural pulse-checker of the group. The individual may be called on to lead the drive, enthusiasm and dynamic nature of the group. The person in this role keeps the group positive and focused on welcoming new members, ensuring the ease of belonging and inclusion, and leading celebrations and acknowledgment of individual and team efforts.

***

Now that we've created our happy bubble of high performance in our close-knit team, how do we replicate that across an organisation? How do we create a giant high-performing team bicycle for an entire organisation that is immune to Power Games?

I'm glad you asked. Let's take a look.

A COLLABORATIVE FUTURE

'The future of leadership on planet, and off planet, is collaborative,' Maja said. She was speaking at an Earth Alliance event as the guest speaker. An avid environmentalist, Maja's announcement that Gaia Enterprises was bidding for the Olympus Project had sent shockwaves through the green community. But they had invited her to share her perspective.

'If we are to contend with the complexities of climate refugees, climate volatility, the effects of tsunamis and rising sea levels, we will need international and multi-disciplined collaborative approaches to find new ways of living and working in our climate ravaged world.'

'But what has the Moon got to do with the Earth?' Someone heckled from the back of the room.

Maja smiled, weary. 'There is no more harsh a climate than the lack of atmosphere in space. If we can build a community facility that allows humans to not only survive but also thrive, we can apply that technology here back on Earth. That's why for the first time we are opening the doors to candidates outside of Gaia graduates. We will build this future for all of us, together.'

CHAPTER 14

HEALTHY POWER STRUCTURES IN ORGANISATIONS

As I've highlighted a few times through this book, the structures and systems within an organisation or team often allow the rise of Power Games to go unchecked. In the previous chapter, I introduced the concepts of triangles and circles in relation to team structure. How healthy – or unhealthy – these structures and systems are within organisations also comes down to triangles and circles.

The following figure highlights the different organisational approaches between triangle and circle structures.

Systems and approaches within triangle versus circle organisational structures

	Triangles	Circles
Expression	Command	Connection
Purpose	Amass	Amplify
Implementation	Push	Grow
Structure	Bricks	Fractals
Dynamic	Hierarchy	Holacracy
Effect	**Energising**	**Enduring**
Characteristic	**Risky**	**Resilient**

Let's consider these differences in a little more detail.

Circles versus Triangles

Triangles are traditional top–down, hierarchical organisations. Decision-makers and authority at the top: a Crown at the pinnacle of the triangle. An org chart is typically represented in this way: the CEO and Board at the top, and everyone below them. This depiction reinforces notions of authority, power and status. That may or may not be helpful, depending on the rest of the structures the business has implemented for the flow of tasks and duties. (Refer to the previous chapter for more on structures.)

Circles allow for collaboration and cooperation. They have flatter hierarchies and can numb the temptation for Power Games, if the systems are designed well.

At the foundations of each of these power structures are beliefs around the purpose and fulfilment of the entity's goals.

Towering triangles

Triangle organisations believe that *command* by a few is the best way forward, for the following reasons:

- Command gives clarity.
- Control builds wealth.
- Together, we push forward.
- Brick by brick we build a tower: everyone has their place.
- One path, one mission, one step at a time.

Classic triangle organisations include the military and para-military agencies, public service, mining and resource companies, and utilities. Wherever a need to harness a lot of people and materials exists, this structure will often be used to keep control. Examples of triangle organisations include:

- the Australian Defence Force (ADF)
- the Australian Federal Police (AFP)

- State Emergency Services (SES)
- government departments (for example, the Department of Home Affairs or Australian Taxation Office)
- mining and resource companies (for example, Rio Tinto or BHP)
- utilities (for example, energy, water or transport companies).

Highly regulated industries that require high compliance for safety and other reasons require strong triangle-based structures.

Interestingly, these hierarchies also include elements of circle structures at the coal face, where decision-making needs to be made live and in the field to make safe, timely decisions, such as on covert military operations. Workers have no time to send a request up the chain when threats are imminent.

Collaborating circles

Circle organisations believe that *connection* of the many is the best way forward, for the following reasons:

- Connection expands perspective.
- Inclusion amplifies ideas and resources: more for all.
- Together, we grow stronger, like strands of a rope woven together.
- Bit by bit, we weave a tapestry: everything is connected.
- Many voices, many truths, multiple paths.

Circle organisations include cooperatives, community banks and social enterprises. Some cooperative organisations are also member-owned and operated, using a more democratic, member-driven model where decision-making is shared among members rather than concentrated at the top. An example is Co-operative Bulk Handling (CBH Group), based in Western Australia. CBH Group is a farmer-owned cooperative and one of the largest grain handlers in the country. As CBH Group explain on their website,

> *Co-operatives are organisations that are owned, controlled and used by their members. They exist to deliver benefits to their members and are based on the values of self-help, self-responsibility, democracy, equality, equity and solidarity.*

Democratic DAOs

And then we have these weird new creatures: DAOs – decentralised autonomous organisations. DAOs are a revolutionary model of governance enabled by blockchain technology, where decision-making is decentralised and driven by community consensus rather than a central authority. DAOs operate through smart contracts – self-executing code on the blockchain that governs organisational rules and actions – ensuring transparency and autonomy.

In a DAO, members typically hold governance tokens, which provide voting rights on key decisions, such as funding allocations, operational changes and strategic initiatives. Examples of DAOs range from investment-focused entities to service-based or protocol-governing organisations. While DAOs offer benefits such as 'trustless' governance[16], inclusivity and operational efficiency, they also face challenges, including legal ambiguity, potential security risks and decision-making complexities due to decentralised coordination. As DAOs continue to evolve, they are shaping new ways of organising and governing enterprises, particularly in finance, technology and social impact sectors.

DAOs are still slow to gain traction. I've been monitoring a social one, Friends with Benefits, for a couple of years now. It uses blockchain technology to create memberships with tokens that are used to vote and nominate funds for different activities, such as social gatherings or creative collaborations. A small

---

16 DAOs are considered 'trustless' or not needing trust to operate because all decisions are transparent and cannot be changed once recorded in the blockchain. We don't need to trust the executive to do the right thing because it will be obvious if they don't. The blockchain technology makes it harder for individuals to swindle or hide outcomes, transactions or decisions.

community of people is driving these activities, so a tiny triangle is emerging. Plus, to gain entry to the club, you need to demonstrate contribution to the community to then be provided with tokens (Coin, anyone?!). I'm imagining more tokens equals more influence – quantifying Coin in a way that has been informal everywhere else.

Will DAOs manage to avoid Power Games due to their radical transparency and decentralised structure? Watch this space.

What's better – circles or triangles?

Each of these primary modes has benefits and drawbacks: Triangles are energising with the unilateral push towards one destination. Triangles, however, are also risky for those in command. When one wears the Crown, unless power is shared, people covet the authority and control, and Power Games have a habit of creeping into the fray. It's tempting to topple the top of a triangle.

Circles, however, are enduring because connections create strength. While a single thread is weak on its own, woven together multiple strands create a solid rope. Even if a single thread is cut, the rest hold fast. Circle structures are also messy, chaotic and harder to wrangle in a time-effective way. And they are not immune to Power Games. In the absence of good structures within a circle organisation, people will still jostle for power.

Resilient organisations – ones that will survive the turbulence ahead – are *connected*, not just *commanded*.

Ultimately, we need circles and triangles, and solid high-performing team bicycles to keep Power Games from taking root in our garden.

Organisational structure and culture

The relationship between power and organisational culture is deeply interconnected, because the way power is distributed and exercised within an organisation shapes its values, norms and behaviours. Here's a breakdown of how these two elements interact within triangle and circle structures.

Culture in triangle hierarchical power structures

In organisations with rigid hierarchies where power is concentrated at the top, the culture tends to be more formal, rule-bound and authoritarian. Decision-making is typically top–down, and employees may feel less able to express ideas or challenge authority. The organisation is usually represented using an organisational chart, with power and authority concentrated at the top of the triangle.

Without attention to systems, this structure can create a culture where conformity is prioritised and innovation is stifled. In some traditional bureaucratic organisations, where power is centralised, the culture may be focused on maintaining order, control and efficiency. Employees in these organisations may be less likely to question leadership or take initiative.

Culture in circle decentralised power structures

Organisations that distribute power more evenly, often through flatter hierarchies or team-based structures, tend to have cultures that emphasise collaboration, innovation and autonomy. Employees in these environments are often encouraged to share ideas, challenge the status quo and participate in decision-making processes.

Companies such as Google or Spotify, which are known for their flatter hierarchies, foster a culture of openness and innovation. Power is often distributed among cross-functional teams, and employees have a higher degree of autonomy.

Organisational structure and employee behaviour

Employee behaviour is also influenced by company structures in place.

Fear and intimidation in triangle cultures

When power is used coercively – through micromanagement, fear of punishment or authoritarian control – an organisational culture of fear and compliance develops. Employees in such cultures may avoid taking risks, sharing ideas or offering constructive criticism, which can lead to low morale and reduced innovation.

In organisations where leaders frequently use threats of job loss or punishment to maintain control, such as some highly competitive financial firms, the culture becomes fear-driven. Employees may prioritise pleasing the boss over making meaningful contributions to the organisation.

Autonomy and engagement in circle cultures

When leaders share their power with employees through delegation, scope for autonomy and the resources they need to succeed, they foster a culture of engagement and accountability. Employees in circle cultures are more likely to feel valued and motivated to contribute to the organisation's success.

In companies where leaders share leadership, such as Southwest Airlines, power is used to support employees, which creates a culture of trust and engagement. This type of culture leads to higher job satisfaction and improved performance.

Organisational structure and cultural norms

Organisational culture reinforces power dynamics. In organisations with a culture of individualism and competition, reinforced with triangle systems and structures, employees are more likely to engage in power struggles, often competing for recognition or advancement. In contrast, cultures that emphasise teamwork and collaboration – that is, circle structures – often distribute power more evenly and discourage hierarchical dominance.

In highly competitive triangle environments, such as certain law firms or investment banks, employees may engage in Power Games like withholding information or undermining colleagues to gain an advantage. This behaviour is often tolerated, and sometimes even rewarded, as part of the culture.

Organisational structure and innovation

Whether an organisation has a triangle or circle structure can also affect its approach to innovation – including idea-sharing and risk-taking.

Effect on idea-sharing

In highly centralised triangle organisations where decision-making authority is concentrated at the top, innovation can be stifled. Employees may feel discouraged from sharing new ideas because decisions are typically made by a select few. Triangles often prioritise stability and control, which can also discourage risk-taking, a key component of innovation (see the following section).

Employees might avoid suggesting novel ideas out of fear of rejection or punishment, leading to status quo thinking. These environments may be slow to adapt to change or miss out on disruptive innovations.

Decentralised circle power structures are generally more conducive to innovation. In such environments, decision-making is distributed across teams or departments, enabling employees at various levels to contribute to creative solutions. This approach encourages a more collaborative and participatory culture, where ideas flow freely. Decentralised power structures can encourage cross-functional collaboration, which can lead to more diverse and innovative ideas. When employees have more autonomy, they are more likely to take ownership of their ideas and experiment without fear of reprimand.

Companies such as Google and 3M have decentralised innovation models, where employees are encouraged to spend a portion of their time working on independent projects. This has led to groundbreaking products, including Gmail and Post-it Notes.

Effect on risk-taking

In organisations with a high power distance – that is, the distance between decision-making at the top of the triangle and at the bottom is long – subordinates are less likely to challenge authority. Employees may fear proposing bold or unconventional ideas because they don't want to risk negative repercussions or criticism from leadership. This fear can inhibit risk-taking. In these environments, employees may stick to safe, incremental innovations rather than pursuing radical changes. Over time, the organisation may fall behind more agile competitors.

Traditional industries, such as finance or government, are often risk averse and prefer incremental changes due to the high stakes involved and the hierarchical nature of these sectors.

In contrast, organisations where employees feel able to take risks without fear of punishment, with clear structures for experiments, accountabilities and responsibilities, tend to be more innovative. Power is used to create a psychologically safe environment where failures are seen as learning opportunities.

Encouraging experimentation fosters a culture of continuous improvement. When employees feel supported by leadership, they are more likely to test new ideas and innovate, even in uncertain conditions.

Amazon is known for embracing a risk-taking culture. CEO Jeff Bezos has said that 'failure and invention are inseparable twins'. This mindset allows Amazon to pursue bold innovations, such as its cloud computing division AWS (Amazon Web Services), which started as a risky experiment.

You can have risk-taking in both triangle and circle organisations, so long as the structures and systems are clear and permissive.

Organisational structure and leadership style

Leaders who prefer an authoritarian style are attracted to triangle structures. They can more easily make decisions unilaterally, without input from their teams, which can discourage creativity and the free flow of ideas.

Leaders who prefer a collaborative style are attracted to circle structures. They use their power to inspire and motivate employees to think creatively. They encourage their teams to challenge the status quo and push boundaries.

These transformational leaders create an environment where innovation is a shared goal, and employees are encouraged to take initiative. Satya Nadella, CEO of Microsoft, is a great example. He reshaped the company's culture to encourage agility, innovation and collaboration. The ensuing focus on the cloud, acquisitions and AI revitalised Microsoft and ensured its continued dominance in the tech space.

Many tech companies adopt a circle ethos to turbocharge innovation. And yet, the leaders can still fall prey to Power Games. (I'm looking at you, Elon.)

Power influences innovation through the way it is distributed and exercised within organisations. Through decentralised decision-making, encouraging risk-taking, and implementing structures that foster idea flow and experiments, innovation can thrive. Leaders play a pivotal role in shaping the power dynamics that either enable or inhibit creativity. To foster a culture of innovation, power must be shared, and employees must feel able to experiment and contribute ideas without fear of repercussions. Even so, a great transformational leader, unhampered by good systems, can still turn tyrant.

Structure as an organisation grows

As an organisation grows, power typically shifts from centralised, informal decision-making in small groups to decentralised, formalised hierarchies with middle management. This shift can increase efficiency and manage complexity, but it also introduces challenges such as hierarchy, bureaucracy, slower decision-making, and potential disengagement from employees who feel further from the power centre. For leaders, balancing formal structures with agility and empowering decentralised teams is crucial for maintaining organisational growth and innovation. The balance of triangles and circles can be managed with clear structure, developing strengths and ensuring safety, as outlined in the previous chapter. Vigilance is required to make sure things don't fall to Power Games through lack of clarity.

Remember: build a culture of inclusion and collaboration, and then create clear structures. It's circles before triangles.

Solving systemic power challenges

Addressing systemic challenges that contribute to the abuse of power requires a multi-faceted approach that tackles underlying cultural, structural and policy issues. Here are some solutions.

Implement strong accountability and oversight mechanisms

Consider the following:

- Create independent oversight bodies, audit committees and internal review processes that hold individuals accountable for their actions, particularly those in leadership roles.

- Conduct regular audits, have clear reporting lines and use unbiased third-party evaluations to help expose and correct abuses of power. Transparency in decision-making is crucial.

- Create an ethics committee or ombudsmen responsible for overseeing how decisions are made and ensuring they meet ethical standards. These bodies serve as an independent party to whom employees can report unethical behaviour without fear of reprisal.

- Ensure you have an ethical Code of Conduct in place. A clear, codified set of ethical guidelines that leaders must follow can act as a reference point for behaviour and decision-making. This code should outline the expectations for the responsible use of power and the consequences of violations.

Foster a transparent and inclusive culture

Encourage an inclusive culture with the following:

- Encourage transparency and openness in communication, ensuring that decisions, policies and promotions are based on merit and are clear to everyone in the organisation.

- Implement processes where decisions, particularly at the executive level, are transparent, documented and shared across the organisation. This could include open meetings or accessible meeting minutes for major strategic decisions.

- Make financial performance, budgeting and executive compensation information open and more transparent to the entire organisation. Regular updates on how funds are being used can build trust and reduce suspicion.

- Ensure all communication channels are pervasive, frequent and open. Share the organisation's updates, key decisions, challenges and triumphs on as many communication platforms as possible to minimise assumptions and gossip. Create 'listening circles' where managers can listen to the challenges and concerns of employees, and then commit to addressing these concerns to close the feedback loop.

- Conduct regular training on ethical leadership and on diversity, equity and inclusion (DEI) initiatives to reduce systemic bias and promote fairness.

Strengthen legal protections for whistleblowers

Ideally, governments as well as organisations should ensure that whistleblowers are legally protected from retaliation, thus encouraging employees to report misconduct without fear of losing their jobs or facing legal consequences. Here's how to protect whistleblowers in your organisation:

- Develop and enforce a strong code of ethics that applies to everyone, from the CEO to entry-level staff. This should clearly define acceptable behaviour, especially regarding power dynamics.

- Create safe, anonymous channels for employees to report unethical behaviour, such as a whistleblower hotline. This encourages people to speak up without fear of retaliation.
- Ensure that robust legal protections are in place across the organisation to protect whistleblowers from retaliation. Make it clear that whistleblowing is seen as a positive contribution to the organisation's integrity.
- Establish a strong, independent board of directors or oversight body with clear responsibilities for monitoring leadership behaviour. These bodies should not be afraid to question or challenge the CEO or senior leadership when needed.
- Ensure that HR and legal functions within the organisation operate independently of senior leadership influence. These departments should have the power to investigate complaints, enforce policies and recommend corrective actions when ethical violations are found.
- Enforce legal frameworks to safeguard those who report abuses of power. In Australia, these include:
  - *Public Interest Disclosure Act 2013* (PID Act): This act provides protections for whistleblowers in the Australian public sector.[17]
  - *Corporations Act 2001*: This act includes provisions for whistleblower protections in the private sector.[18]

  Each Australian state and territory also has its own whistleblower protection laws, including:

  - Australian Capital Territory: *Public Interest Disclosure Act 2012*

---

17 See www.legislation.gov.au/C2013A00133/latest/text for the full Act.
18 See www.legislation.gov.au/C2004A00818/latest/text.

- New South Wales: *Public Interest Disclosures Act 2022*
- Northern Territory: *Public Interest Disclosure Act 2008*
- Queensland: *Public Interest Disclosure Act 2010*
- South Australia: *Public Interest Disclosure Act 2018*
- Tasmania: *Public Interest Disclosures Act 2002*
- Victoria: *Public Interest Disclosures Act 2012*
- Western Australia: *Public Interest Disclosure Act 2003*.

Flatten hierarchical structures with more circles

Move away from rigid hierarchical models and towards more decentralised structures that distribute decision-making power and responsibility across teams. Flattening the hierarchy reduces the concentration of power and the potential for abuse.

Implement team-based or collaborative leadership models where leadership is shared and employees have more input in decision-making.

Cultivate ethical leadership

Prioritise ethical leadership by hiring and promoting leaders who demonstrate integrity, empathy and accountability.

Integrate ethical decision-making into leadership training programs and establish clear ethical guidelines that leaders are expected to follow.

Use 360-degree feedback tools to assess a leader's impact on employees and encourage self-reflection on their use of power. Though these processes are sometimes flawed, where any negative feedback becomes a witch hunt, developing a comprehensive matrix-style approach to feedback ensures multiple perspectives are gained on an individual's impact, reducing the opportunity for gaslighting and other manipulation tactics.

Address power imbalances in employment contracts

Reform employment agreements that disproportionately favour employers, such as non-compete clauses or forced arbitration, which can prevent employees from seeking justice or leaving toxic environments.

Promote diversity and inclusion

Address systemic discrimination by promoting diversity and inclusion across all levels of the organisation. Diverse leadership teams are less likely to engage in groupthink or perpetuate discriminatory practices.

Implement comprehensive DEI policies, ensure diversity in hiring, and track the progress of underrepresented groups in leadership roles.

Legal reforms for executive accountability

Strengthen legal frameworks that hold executives accountable for corporate misconduct. This could include more stringent penalties for corporate malfeasance or personal liability for executives who fail to prevent systemic abuses.

Implement ethical AI and data use policies

In a world increasingly driven by technology, organisations need ethical guidelines on the use of data and artificial intelligence (AI) – otherwise, abuses of power (for example, surveillance and biased algorithms) can quickly develop.

Establish clear policies on data privacy, AI ethics and the use of technology in decision-making processes, ensuring that power is not centralised in data-rich entities.

***

Addressing systemic challenges across your organisation requires a holistic approach that combines leadership accountability, transparency, legal reforms and cultural shifts. These changes promote fairness, reduce the potential for abuse and help ensure that organisations foster environments of ethical leadership and shared responsibility. Continuous reflection and adaptation are crucial as new systemic issues emerge.

So – how are you feeling? You've developed the Four Spheres of Power for yourself and others. You've built one or more high-performing team bicycles. And now you've led the way for transparent and inclusive deployment of power across an organisation. #legend

Before you congratulate yourself too much, let's check if you've missed any weeds in your culture garden. Turn the page and see what might still be lurking.

CHAPTER 15

SEVEN DEADLY SINS OF SYSTEMS POWER ABUSE

Think you've done a good job of creating circles and triangles within your team and organisation? The culture is inclusive and safe, and the processes are clear?

Abuse of power might still take root in your culture garden. Systemic issues might still be lurking that you are not aware of: problems embedded within the structures, policies and culture of your organisation or institution, making the abuse of power easier or even enabling it.

In this chapter, I outline the systemic issues that can lead to or perpetuate abuse of power.

Lack of accountability and oversight

Watch out for the following:

- No clear accountability structures for leadership behaviour or decision-making. Leaders are rarely questioned, and no systems are in place to hold them accountable.

- Frequent policy exceptions for top leadership, where rules apply selectively or are bypassed altogether for those in power.

- Individuals in power feel emboldened to abuse their authority, because no consequences exist for their actions.

Hierarchical organisational structures and top-down decision-making

Check for these issues:

- Lower-ranking employees with little input or influence, and decisions made without transparency.

- Centralised decision-making where all critical decisions are made by a small group of people, often behind closed doors, with little or no consultation with others.

- Absence of feedback loops or mechanisms for employees to question decisions or voice concerns without fear of retaliation.

- A culture of obedience and deference to authority, making it harder for employees to challenge or report abuses.

Toxic workplace culture

The following can really allow Power Games to thrive:

- The culture rewards aggressive competition or cutthroat tactics over collaboration, leading to bullying, manipulation and exploitation.

- Results are prioritised over ethics.

- Leaders promote close friends or family members, regardless of competence, or give special treatment to individuals within a tight inner circle.

- Preferential treatment exists in terms of perks, benefits or workloads for a select few, creating an uneven playing field.

- High levels of fear or intimidation exist within the organisation, and employees are afraid to speak up, challenge leadership or raise issues.

- Frequent retaliation is seen against employees who attempt to report misconduct or speak out against leadership.

- Hero worship of the CEO or key leaders is excessive, where they are seen as infallible and untouchable, and any criticism is immediately shut down.
- Leaders are never challenged by their peers, board members or even shareholders, often leading to unchecked decision-making power.
- Loyalty is to individuals rather than the organisation, and people are rewarded for their allegiance to those in power rather than for performance or merit.
- Any disloyalty, or even minor dissent, is punished, with leaders cultivating an 'us versus them' mentality.
- The leadership succession plan is unclear and leaders stay in their roles indefinitely, creating an environment where new ideas and voices are stifled.
- Grooming or promoting talent from within the organisation is not encouraged, often to protect the power base of those at the top.
- The churn in middle management is constant, as those who might push back against power imbalances or unethical behaviour often find themselves forced out or voluntarily leaving due to toxic culture.
- Employee engagement and satisfaction is low, with surveys (if conducted) showing that people feel disempowered or undervalued.
- Echo chambers exist, with no dissenting opinions or perspectives sought, and the leadership team defaulting to confirmation bias to reinforce their own point of view.

Poor reporting mechanisms

Also watch out for these bad signs:
- Inadequate whistleblowing policies or a lack of anonymous reporting channels prevent employees from safely reporting

misconduct. Even when policies exist, they may not be enforced, or whistleblowers may face retaliation.

- Financial management and budgeting processes are opaque and lack transparency, with employees and even middle management having no idea how money is being spent or allocated.

- Hiring and promotion practices are secretive, and decisions on who advances are not based on merit but on favouritism, cronyism or unclear criteria.

- Internal mechanisms for complaints don't exist. With weak or non-existent whistleblower protections, individuals who report unethical behaviour face retribution or are ignored.

- HR or compliance departments are not capable of independently investigating power abuse claims, often leading to a lack of serious action on complaints.

- Feedback from employees never reaches decision-makers, or when it does, it is filtered to align with the preferences of those in power.

- No mechanisms exist for constructive dialogue, leaving employees feeling unheard or disregarded when they raise issues.

- Employees are discouraged from reporting abuses of power, and perpetrators are emboldened by the absence of consequences.

The Harvey Weinstein scandal revealed how poor reporting structures and fear of retaliation allowed sexual harassment and misconduct to go unchecked for years, even as many within the industry were aware of the behaviour.

Power imbalances in employment contracts

The following are also red flags:

- Certain employment contracts, such as those with non-compete clauses or mandatory arbitration agreements, limit employees' ability to challenge wrongful terminations, harassment or discrimination. These clauses often protect employers from lawsuits.

- Employees with limited legal recourse are less likely to report abuse or seek justice, allowing powerful individuals to act with impunity.

Systemic discrimination

Watch out for the following discriminatory process:

- Institutionalised discrimination based on race, gender or other characteristics, which can create environments where certain groups are systematically disadvantaged. This discrimination often leads to unequal pay, lack of opportunities and a higher likelihood of being targeted for abuse.

- Homogeneous leadership teams, both in terms of demographics and thinking, leading to lack of diversity in thought. When decision-makers all look, think or act the same, dissenting voices and innovative ideas are discouraged.

- Groupthink mentality, where dissent is actively discouraged, and people are expected to conform to the views of those in power.

- Marginalised groups becoming more vulnerable to exploitation, with fewer resources to challenge the status quo.

Studies show that women and minorities in many corporate environments face a 'glass ceiling', where their opportunities for advancement are limited, and they are more likely to face discriminatory behaviour or harassment without recourse.

Profit-driven prioritisation

Finally, watch out for these issues:

- Profit is prioritised over ethics, with incentives provided for leaders to cut corners, mistreat employees or engage in illegal practices to achieve short-term financial goals.

- Ethical considerations are sidelined in favour of financial gain, leading to exploitation and abuses that go unpunished if they contribute to the bottom line.

Amazon, for example, has faced criticism for pushing warehouse workers to extreme limits in the name of efficiency and profit, resulting in unsafe working conditions and mistreatment.

***

Systemic issues that foster abuse of power typically arise from weak accountability structures, rigid hierarchies, toxic cultures and legal frameworks that protect those in authority. Addressing these problems requires comprehensive reforms, including creating more transparent systems, promoting ethical leadership and enforcing policies that enable individuals to challenge abuses without fear of retaliation.

Phew! It's been a lot of work to get this far. Being a good human requires a lot of patience and persistence. We've seen how some bad actors can rise up and take advantage of others within a weak system. And, even with all our efforts, we can still feel powerless in the face of oppression.

And what then?

Let's see what it takes to speak truth to power.

CHAPTER 16

SPEAKING TRUTH TO POWER

Alexei Navalny died in a Siberian prison, most likely at the behest of Russian President, Vladimir Putin. That's what autocrats do: they rid themselves of opposition. In Putin's Russia, if you speak truth to power, you die. It's the heady stuff of great espionage novels. But it's real life – real lives, gone.

How does one develop Alexei Navalny's incredible courage? He returned to Russia after surviving a poisoning attempt, knowing he would be arrested and possibly killed. *Spoiler alert:* He was. He believed in fighting for democracy, freedom and a fair Russia. He sacrificed his life for the cause.

How can we prevent this kind of power abuse and the squashing of freedoms in our own part of the planet? We can start in our own backyard.

Ever the hopeful optimist, I believe we can fight against these nefarious practices, starting within our own teams and our own organisations.

Learning how to speak truth to power

To speak truth to power, start with yourself. When do you feel powerful? Have you ever felt a secret thrill telling someone what to do, denying someone's wish or even breaking a few rules?

These are the seeds of temptation. Be careful what you nurture. Don't become the thing you rail against.

Here's how to build an immune system to the abuses of power:

- Start with building *courage* in yourself and others. Encourage a sense of agency, and adopt the posture of being an independent thinker, a go-getter, and a responsible and accountable person. With others, ask their opinion, encourage critique and celebrate individual wins. Stoke your Cauldron of Courage, and encourage others to do the same.

- Then expand *status* and credibility in yourself and others. Develop expertise, skills and knowledge. Become a valuable contributor and connector, problem-solver and trend spotter. Fill your Coin bag, and that of others, to bursting to get taken seriously.

- Next develop *influence*. You can go two ways: recruiting others to follow your will, or recruiting others based on your shared values for a collective effort towards a better world. One is the dark path that leads towards empire building and abuse of power; the other is the light side of the Force, where we are stronger together and look out for one another. When you blow into that Conch, let it be a clarion call for a better world.

- And, finally, if you're granted a lofty Crown, it's your chance to change the game.

Build your high-performing team bicycle. Tend to your culture garden. Develop power structures and systems that are transparent and accountable.

No one hero will save the day. But we are all heroes if we follow our values and think of the greater good.

With such a movement, one based on values and with no one lone hero, if our enemies strive to cut down our spokespeople, more can rise to serve that role. Vision and values carry us, a collective force, towards our better future.

'You are not allowed to give up ... If they decide to kill me, it means that we are incredibly strong', said Navalny, two years before he was allegedly murdered.

With an autocrat, when we cut down a snake, it's not a hydra; the cult of personality ends with the snake – so long as we reclaim the systems from triangles as much as we can, and bring them back to circles.

Our chief concern should be, 'How do I build agency, autonomy and authority in more of my people so more of us can work on building a better future?' When we consider 'circles before triangles', or 'all of us before myself alone', we're starting to fight the intoxicating mess that is power.

Rising up to change power systems from within is a risky business. We put our jobs, our reputation and our relationships on the line. For some, like Alexei Navalny, that also means putting our life on the line.

Is it worth it?

Consider what's at stake: time and time again, in speaking with leaders about their experiences on the receiving end of Power Games, they've cited stress, anxiety, despair, crippling self-doubt, frustration, trauma and betrayal. The more we call out abuses of power, or at least the bending of power, the better able we will be to craft a healthy expression of it. For that, we need courage and conviction like Alexei Navalny's. Vale, brave man. May we all find the strength to build a life, a team, an organisation, a political system that honours integrity and compassion in service to a better world.

Play the game?

Let's change the game.

WHAT'S NEXT?

Thank you for your efforts on reading right through to the end of this book. Of course, this is not the end, but the beginning for you. It's time to implement – and I've got some ideas for what you can do next.

First, pick up the additional bonus resources for this book here, including https://www.zoerouth.com/power-games-bonus-material.

Next, get ongoing insights on the future of leadership by listening to my podcast, *The Future of Leadership*, or by reading one of my blogs – the Fit for the Future Leadership eJournal and Bookish, on all things books. You can find these on my website under the Podcast, Blog and Books tabs.

Need a guiding hand to implement these ideas with your team? I love facilitating strategy, culture and collaboration workshops. Just email me zoe@zoerouth.com to discuss your challenges and opportunities. You can also find more info on my website.

Want to find out how the Gaia characters navigate Power Games in a climate-ravaged future on Earth and the Moon and beyond? Dive into the award-winning books, starting with *The Olympus Project*.

Lastly, if this book was useful to you, I'd dance with happiness if you leave a review on Goodreads or Amazon or email me directly. Reviews make a huge difference to the book's discoverability – and the more people learn how to use power well in businesses, the better off we will all be. One or two sentences about what was most useful or interesting to you is all that's needed. Thanks in advance for the gift of your time and energy.

In the meantime, live with grace, lead in service.

Zoë

APPENDIX A

SAMPLE CODE OF ETHICS

1. **Purpose statement:** Outline the purpose of the Code of Ethics. For example:

    'Our Code of Ethics serves to guide our behaviour and decisions in a manner that reflects our values, integrity and commitment to our community.'

2. **Core values:**

    - *Integrity:* Honesty, transparency and accountability in all actions.

    - *Respect:* Treat everyone with dignity, compassion and fairness.

    - *Responsibility:* Uphold obligations to stakeholders, the environment and future generations.

    - *Excellence:* Strive for high-quality service, continuous improvement and innovation.

    - *Inclusivity:* Foster diversity and support equity in every facet of our work.

3. **Key principles:**

    - *Respect for individuals:* Commit to treating everyone with respect, valuing diversity, and ensuring an environment free from discrimination or harassment.

- *Fairness and transparency:* Make decisions openly and fairly, ensuring all actions are justifiable and without conflicts of interest.

- *Confidentiality:* Protect sensitive information about clients, employees, partners and other stakeholders.

- *Responsibility to the community:* Engage with and contribute positively to the community, understanding that our actions have a lasting impact.

- *Environmental stewardship:* Commit to sustainable practices that protect the environment for future generations.

4. **Standards of conduct:**

    - *Professional conduct:* Maintain professionalism in interactions with all stakeholders.

    - *Conflict of interest:* Avoid situations where personal interests conflict with professional duties.

    - *Health and safety:* Prioritise the safety and wellbeing of employees, clients and the community.

    - *Honesty and integrity in communication:* Ensure truthful, accurate and respectful communication at all times.

    - *Ethical use of resources:* Use resources responsibly, minimising waste and prioritising sustainable options.

5. **Compliance and accountability:**

    - *Legal compliance:* Abide by all applicable laws and regulations.

    - *Reporting violations:* Encourage a culture where employees and stakeholders feel safe reporting unethical behaviour without fear of retaliation.

    - *Consequences of violations:* Define the process for handling ethical breaches, including disciplinary actions as necessary.

6. **Commitment to continuous improvement:**
   - Regularly review and update the Code of Ethics to adapt to new challenges, ensuring it remains relevant and effective.
   - Provide training and resources for employees to understand and integrate the Code of Ethics into their daily responsibilities.

APPENDIX B

SAMPLE CODE OF CONDUCT

Purpose

This Code of Conduct sets out the standards of behaviour expected from all members of *[organisation name]*, including staff, volunteers, contractors and stakeholders. We are committed to fostering a respectful, inclusive and professional environment where all individuals feel valued and can contribute meaningfully.

1. **Respect and inclusion:**

    - Treat all colleagues, clients and stakeholders with respect, dignity and fairness.

    - Embrace diversity and strive to create an inclusive environment free from discrimination, harassment or bullying.

    - Communicate openly, honestly and constructively with others, avoiding disrespectful or aggressive language or behaviour.

2. **Integrity and professionalism:**

    - Act with integrity and honesty in all interactions, and maintain the organisation's reputation.

    - Avoid conflicts of interest, disclosing any personal interests that may affect decisions.

    - Maintain professionalism in work and interactions, including using professional language, attire and behaviour.

3. **Confidentiality and data protection:**
   - Respect the confidentiality of sensitive information, including but not limited to organisational data, client information and proprietary knowledge.
   - Protect personal and sensitive information in compliance with data protection laws and organisational policies.
   - Report any data breaches or incidents promptly to the appropriate department.

4. **Accountability:**
   - Take responsibility for actions, decisions and their impact on the organisation and its stakeholders.
   - Report any behaviour that violates this Code of Conduct or other policies of the organisation.
   - Seek guidance from managers or supervisors if unsure of the correct course of action.

5. **Health, safety and wellbeing:**
   - Follow all health and safety protocols to maintain a safe working environment.
   - Actively contribute to creating a supportive and positive workplace culture.
   - Take care of personal physical and mental wellbeing, and respect the wellbeing of others.

6. **Compliance with laws and policies:**
   - Comply with all relevant laws, regulations and organisational policies.
   - Avoid any activity that could be interpreted as illegal or unethical.
   - Report any suspected or actual violations of the law, regulations or organisational policies.

7. **Use of organisational resources:**

    - Use organisational resources responsibly and only for legitimate business purposes.

    - Avoid misuse of organisational property, such as equipment, funds and facilities.

    - Respect intellectual property rights and ensure that any organisational materials are used appropriately.

8. **Ethical leadership and abuse of power:**

    - *Definition of abuse of power:* Abuse of power involves using one's authority to intimidate, coerce or gain unfair personal advantage. This includes actions such as favouritism, unfair treatment and using influence to silence differing views.

    - *Expectations for ethical leadership:* Leaders are role models and are expected to use their authority to empower, not intimidate. Treat all employees fairly, promote inclusivity and make decisions transparently.

    - *Zero tolerance for bullying, harassment and intimidation:* Bullying and harassment, whether overt (like shouting) or subtle (such as excluding someone from opportunities), are forms of abuse. The organisation is committed to maintaining a workplace free of intimidation.

    - *Conflict of interest and personal gain:* Using one's position to gain personal benefits (such as favours or promotions) is unacceptable. All conflicts of interest must be disclosed to prevent biased decision-making.

    - *Transparency and accountability:* Leaders must act transparently, document decisions and be open to scrutiny. This ensures decisions affecting others are fair and justified.

    - *Fairness in decision-making:* Decisions should be merit-based and free from personal bias. Leaders should distribute resources, opportunities and rewards equitably.

- *Handling of grievances and complaints:* The organisation provides a safe, anonymous channel for reporting abuse of power. All complaints will be handled with care, and whistleblowers will be protected.
- *Respectful communication:* Authority does not grant the right to demean others. All interactions should be respectful and professional, regardless of rank.
- *Prohibition of favouritism and nepotism:* Preferential treatment is not permitted in hiring, promotions or other workplace dynamics. Transparency ensures fairness and merit-based advancement.
- *Training on power dynamics:* Training on power dynamics, ethical leadership and the prevention of abuse is available to all employees to promote a healthy work environment.
- *Responsibility to enable others:* Leaders are expected to enable team members to contribute ideas and feel safe challenging opinions without fear of retribution.
- *Procedures for addressing and preventing retaliation:* Retaliation against those who report misconduct or abuse of power will not be tolerated. Specific consequences are outlined for retaliatory behaviour.

9. **Continuous improvement:**
   - Engage in ongoing learning and development to enhance skills and contribute to the organisation's goals.
   - Offer constructive feedback and suggestions to improve organisational practices and outcomes.
   - Be open to receiving feedback as a tool for personal and professional growth.

Enforcement

Violations of this Code of Conduct may lead to disciplinary action, up to and including termination of employment or association with the organisation, in accordance with organisational policies.

Acknowledgment

All members of our organisation are expected to read, understand and adhere to this Code of Conduct. By signing below, you acknowledge your commitment to uphold the standards and principles outlined above.

APPENDIX C

COLLABORATION HANDBOOK QUESTIONS

My profile is: *[DiSC/Myers Briggs/HBDI/Values/Leadership Maturity]*

My core strength or superpower is:

My (known) blind spot is:

I am currently working on improving:

If you want to treat me with respect:

How I prefer to receive difficult feedback:

A pet peeve of mine is:

How you can tell if I am frustrated:

I work best in the: *[morning/afternoon/evening/night]*

One thing I'd like you to know about me is:

How I like to be appreciated:

Meetings work best for me if:

Other bits about me:

APPENDIX D

INTEGRATIVE DECISION-MAKING IN A HOLACRACY

A holacracy (as opposed to, say, a democracy or autocracy) is a self-governing system. It employs a structured decision-making process known as integrative decision-making (IDM), designed to integrate diverse perspectives efficiently without requiring full consensus. This method ensures that decisions are made swiftly while addressing potential objections that could hinder progress.

The IDM process comprises the following steps, as documented at holacracy.org[19]:

1. *Present proposal:* The proposer outlines a specific tension or issue and presents a proposal to address it. This step is conducted without interruption or discussion.

2. *Clarifying questions:* Participants may ask questions to better understand the proposal or the underlying tension. The proposer responds to these questions, but no reactions or opinions are shared at this stage.

3. *Reaction round:* Each participant, except the proposer, shares their initial reactions to the proposal. This is done sequentially, without discussion or responses to others' reactions.

---

[19] Read the full Constitution here: https://www.holacracy.org/constitution/5-0/#art545.

4. *Amend and clarify:* Based on the feedback received, the proposer may amend the proposal to better address the original tension. This step is solely for the proposer to make changes; no discussion is permitted.

5. *Objection round:* Participants are asked if they foresee any reasons why adopting the proposal would cause harm or move the organisation backward. Objections are stated, tested for validity and captured without discussion. If no valid objections arise, the proposal is adopted.

6. *Integration:* For each valid objection, the group collaborates to modify the proposal to resolve the objection while still addressing the original tension. This iterative process continues until all objections are resolved, leading to the adoption of the refined proposal.

This approach ensures that decisions are made efficiently, incorporating diverse viewpoints and addressing concerns without the delays often associated with consensus-based methods. By focusing on resolving specific tensions and integrating objections, Holacracy's IDM process promotes agile and adaptive decision-making within organisations.

FURTHER READING

Barr, Stacey. (2014) *Practical Performance Management: Using the PuMP Blueprint for Fast, Easy and Engaging KPIs*, The PuMP Press.

—— (2017) *Prove It! How to Create a High Performance Culture and Measurable Success*, Wiley.

Brown, Brené. (2016) *Daring Greatly: How the Courage to Be Vulnerable Transforms the Way We Live, Love, Parent and Lead*, Penguin Books.

Cialdini, Robert. (2021) *Influence: The Psychology of Persuasion*, HarperCollins Publishers.

—— (2017) *Pre-Suasion: A Revolutionary Way to Influence and Persuade*, Random House UK.

Connors, Roger, Smith, Tom and Hickman, Craig. (2010) *The Oz Principle: Getting Results through Individual and Organizational Accountability*, Penguin Group USA.

Frankl, Victor. (1946) *Man's Search for Meaning*, 2008 edition published by Random House UK.

Gladwell, Malcolm. (2014) *David and Goliath: Underdogs, Misfits and the Art of Battling Giants*, Penguin Books.

—— (2009) *Outliers: The Story of Success*, Penguin Books.

Grant, Adam. (2014) *Give and Take: Why Helping Others Drives Our Success*, Penguin Books.

Greene, Robert. (2000) *The 48 Rules of Power*, Penguin Books.

Heimans, Jeremy and Timms, Henry. (2018) *New Power: How Power Works in Our Hyperconnected World – and How to Make it Work for You*, Pan Macmillan Australia.

Holiday, Ryan. (2014) *The Obstacle is the Way: The Timeless Art of Turning Trials into Triumph*, Portfolio.

Keltner, Dacher. (2017) *The Power Paradox: How We Gain and Lose Influence*, Penguin Books.

Kotler, Steven. (2023) *The Art of Impossible: A Peak Performance Primer*, HarperCollins Publishers.

Machiavelli, Niccolò. (1532) *The Prince*, 2011 edition published by Penguin Books.

Miki, Megumi. (2019) *Quietly Powerful: How Your Quiet Nature is Your Hidden Leadership Strength*, Major Street.

Nekvapil, Kemi. (2022) *Power: A Woman's Guide to Living and Leading Without Apology*, Penguin Australia.

Pfeffer, Jeffrey. (2022) *7 Rules of Power: Surprising – But True – Advice on How to Get Things Done and Advance Your Career*, Swift Press.

Pink, Daniel. (2009) *Drive: The Surprising Truth About What Motivates Us*, Riverhead.

Robbins, Tony. (2001) *Unlimited Power: The New Science of Personal Achievement*, Simon & Schuster UK.

Robertson, Brian. (2016) *Holacracy: The Revolutionary Management System that Abolishes Hierarchy*, Penguin UK.

Robertson, Rachael. (2013) *Leading on the Edge: Extraordinary Stories and Leadership Insights from the World's Most Extreme Workplace*, John Wiley & Sons Australia.

Routh, Zoë. (2015) *Composure: How Centered Leaders Make the Biggest Difference*, Inner Compass Australia Pty Ltd.

—— (2017) *Moments: Leadership When It Matters Most*, Inner Compass Australia Pty Ltd.

—— (2018) *Loyalty: Stop Unwanted Staff Turnover, Boost Engagement, and Create Lifelong Advocates*, Inner Compass Australia Pty Ltd.

—— (2024) *People Stuff: Beyond Personality Problems, An Advanced Handbook for Leadership*, Inner Compass Australia Pty Ltd.

Sandberg, Sheryl. (2013) *Lean In: Women, Work, and the Will to Lead*, Knopf.

Sinek, Simon. (2017) *Leaders Eat Last: Why Some Teams Pull Together and Others Don't*, Penguin UK.

Slade, Samantha. (2018) *Going Horizontal: Creating a Non-Hierarchical Organization, One Practice at a Time*, Random House US.

Starhawk. (2011) *The Empowerment Manual: A Guide for Collaborative Groups*, New Society Publishers.

Storr, Will. (2023) *The Status Game: On Human Life and How to Play It*, HarperCollins Publishers.

Torbert, William. (2004) *Action Inquiry: The Secret of Timely and Transforming Leadership*, Random House US.

Tzu, Sun. (5th century BC) *The Art of War*, 2009 edition published by Penguin Books.

Van Edwards, Vanessa. (2022) *Cues: Master the Secret Language of Charismatic Communication*, Portfolio.

ACKNOWLEDGMENTS

I have thought about this topic and this book for many years. Power is a huge force in our lives, and yet we harness it so poorly. Too often, we are victims of its misuse and abuse.

I want to thank my clients for their stories and experiences, and the courage to keep leading despite the challenges. I want to thank my blog readers for their insights from a survey I ran as part of the research behind this book. The humbling statistic that 100 per cent of respondents had experienced some form of Power Games in the workplace was sobering.

In particular, I want to thank the following people for giving up their time and energy to recount their experiences of power in the workplace: Olimpia Mazza, Vy Le, Nick Tebbey, Beth Barratt-Browne, Chantal Atkinson, Lisa Dart, Sam Robinson, Sharon (Stokeld) Tuffin and Michelle Chin.

To all the authors whose work I have read and studied to gain clarity and insights, thank you for the efforts and courage you had to put your work out into the world. I am grateful for your wisdom.

To my husband, Rob, thanks for being a continual support and champion of my work. I really couldn't do this authoring without you.

Thanks to the team at Publish Central – including Charlotte Duff, my editor, and Michael Hanrahan, chief book enthusiast – for encouragement and quality work. Thanks also to the amazing

Lynne Cazaly for pulling out the goods for another awesome book cover and wonderful illustrations.

Finally, thank you to you, the reader and leader, for adventuring with me. I wish you courage and grace in nudging the world forward to a better place.

ABOUT THE AUTHOR

Zoë Routh is a leadership futurist, podcaster and multiple award-winning author. She works with leaders and teams to explore what's coming – and what it means for leadership of the future.

She has worked with individuals and teams internationally and in Australia since 1987. From wild Canadian rivers to the Australian Outback and boardroom jungles, Zoë is an adventurist! She facilitates strategy and culture for the future with audacious teams.

Zoë's fourth leadership book, *People Stuff: Beyond Personality Problems – An Advanced Handbook for Leadership*, won the Book of the Year at the Australian Business Book Awards in 2020. Her fifth book, *The Olympus Project*, is a leadership futurist science fiction dystopian novel that won a Gold Medal at the Readers' Favorite Awards in 2023. The second book in the series, *Olympus Bound*, won a Silver Medal in 2024.

Zoë is the producer of *The Future of Leadership* podcast, dedicated to asking 'What if?' and sharing big ideas on what leadership we need now for what's next.

Zoë is an outdoor adventurist who enjoys telemark skiing, has run six marathons, is a one-time belly dancer, has survived cancer, and loves hiking in the high country. She is married to a gorgeous Aussie and is a self-confessed dark chocolate addict.

Find out more at www.zoerouth.com, and contact her via zoe@zoerouth.com.

Other books by Zoë Routh

Leadership non-fiction:

- *Composure: How Centered Leaders Make the Biggest Difference*
- *Moments: Leadership When It Matters Most*
- *Loyalty: Stop Unwanted Staff Turnover, Boost Engagement, and Create Lifelong Advocates*
- *People Stuff: Beyond Personality Problems – An Advanced Handbook for Leadership.*

The Gaia Series (fiction):

- *Terra Blanca Insurrection* (Prequel)
- *The Olympus Project* (Book 1)
- *Olympus Bound* (Book 2)
- *Olympus Rising* (Book 3).

www.ingramcontent.com/pod-product-compliance
Lightning Source LLC
Chambersburg PA
CBHW061206070526
44583CB00025B/3136